MODERN PRESSURE CANNING

RECIPES AND TECHNIQUES FOR
TODAY'S HOME CANNER

AMELIA JEANROY

PHOTOGRAPHY BY KERRY MICHAELS

VOYAGEUR
PRESS

Brimming with creative inspiration, how-to projects, and useful information to enrich your everyday life, Quarto Knows is a favorite destination for those pursuing their interests and passions. Visit our site and dig deeper with our books into your area of interest: Quarto Creates, Quarto Cooks, Quarto Homes, Quarto Lives, Quarto Drives, Quarto Explores, Quarto Gifts, or Quarto Kids.

Photography © Kerry Michaels, except the following from Shutterstock: pages 18 (bottom), 25, 38, 43, 58, 62, 75, 84, 103, 110, 116, 122, 124, 134, 148, 152, 162, 164, 172, 175, 178, 182

First published in 2018 by Voyageur Press, an imprint of The Quarto Group, 401 Second Avenue North, Suite 310, Minneapolis, MN 55401 USA. T (612) 344-8100 F (612) 344-8692 www.QuartoKnows.com

Voyageur Press titles are also available at discount for retail, wholesale, promotional, and bulk purchase. For details, contact the Special Sales Manager by email at specialsales@quarto.com or by mail at The Quarto Group, Attn: Special Sales Manager, 401 Second Avenue North, Suite 310, Minneapolis, MN 55401 USA.

10 9 8 7 6 5 4 3 2 1

ISBN: 978-0-7603-5210-6

Library of Congress Cataloging-in-Publication Data
Names: Jeanroy, Amelia, author.
Title: Modern pressure canning : recipes and techniques for today's home
   canner / Amelia Jeanroy ; photographs by Kerry Michaels.
Description: Minneapolis, MN : Voyageur Press, 2018. | Includes index.
Identifiers: LCCN 2017051171 | ISBN 9780760352106 (paperback)
Subjects: LCSH: Canning and preserving. | Pressure cooking. | BISAC: COOKING
   / Methods / Canning & Preserving. | COOKING / Methods / Special
   Appliances. | COOKING / Methods / General.
Classification: LCC TX603 .J39 2018 | DDC 641.4/2—dc23
LC record available at https://lccn.loc.gov/2017051171

ACQUIRING EDITOR: Todd Berger
PROJECT MANAGER: Alyssa Lochner
ART DIRECTOR: Cindy Samargia Laun
COVER DESIGN: Faceout Studio
PAGE DESIGN AND LAYOUT: Laura Shaw Design

Printed in China

CONTENTS

INTRODUCTION

The glass clinks gently in the hot, soapy water as I wash my jars for this year's canning. Sitting on the counter are colanders full of tomatoes and peppers that need to be saved for the winter. Although canning involves plenty of work, it's something I look forward to every year. Just like cooking dinner, the work is rewarding because of the taste: there's nothing better than opening a jar full of flavor in the middle of winter.

The jump from canning to pressure canning comes at a different point for different people. I decided to take the plunge into pressure canning as my skills grew in the garden. My family was living on a mountain in Montana and most of my entertainment came from growing vegetables and fruit. Although I started canning jams and jellies, it became obvious I needed to be able to preserve much more— and that required pressure canning.

But that's me! Why should *you* learn to pressure can? In short, pressure canning puts the power of food preservation at your fingertips. Whether your inspiration is the farmers' market or a treasured family recipe, you can preserve it. Pressure canning lets you preserve the foods you and your family like to eat so you can enjoy them at their peak, year-round. It's great for the spontaneous cook, who likes to have a variety of ingredients to work with. It's also wonderful for those who want convenience without sacrificing health benefits or taste. Unlike store-bought canned food, there are never any preservatives or questionable ingredients in home-canned food. And you simply can't beat the taste and texture attainable when home canning.

I enjoy teaching people the ins and outs of pressure canning. It's so much fun to walk to the garden with new canners and load up a basket with fruits and veggies. After a couple of hours prepping and canning, we all go home with jars of beautiful preserved food. It's a lesson those new to canning won't soon forget. And it's exciting to share not only a hobby, but a way of life: home cooking from your own pantry. Welcome to *Modern Pressure Canning*.

WHAT IS THE DIFFERENCE BETWEEN PRESSURE CANNING AND WATER BATH CANNING?

Pressure canning and water bath canning are similar in that they are both ways to preserve food in your own kitchen. The general process of putting food in jars, attaching lids, heating to seal, and storing are the same. However, there are some major differences you should know.

All foods have natural acidity levels. Many fruits and tomatoes are highly acidic. These foods can be water bath canned. Or, take pickles: cucumbers (a low-acid food) in an acidic pickling solution. These can also be water bath canned.

Water bath canning, or hot water canning as it's sometimes called, is the method of submerging filled jars into hot water and boiling for a specific period of time. This means the internal temperature of the food in the jars is heated to 212°F. It's a great way to start canning, and the most common way to make popular pantry items such as jams, jellies, and pickles. However, to get a wider range of foods in jars, you need to learn the art of pressure canning, which is what this book covers.

Pressure canning is the preserving method by which filled jars are placed into a large pot with just a few inches of water in it. A locking lid is placed on the pot and steam develops inside the pot. The jars' contents reach an internal temperature of 240°F under a specific pressure (in pounds, see page 29), and the recipe states a specific period of time to hold that pressure. Pressure canning can be used for a wider variety of foods. You can process vegetables and fruits with low or high acidity, meats, poultry, fish, sauces, and even whole recipes—such as soups or stews. Pressure canning generally means less mess, and my jars always seem to seal when I pressure can. (I also admit some bias—I love canning meat. On the farm, we raise much of our own meat, and being able to process it myself means I can fill my pantry with healthy food that has been raised ethically.)

Pressure canning, as you might expect, is done in a *pressure canner*. A pressure canner is a large pot designed specifically for the canning process; do not confuse a pressure *canner* with a pressure *cooker*. A pressure cooker is very useful, but it's a different piece of equipment meant for general cooking. Although there is some crossover, and electric pressure cookers can be used to can a couple of jars at a time, they are two distinctly different kitchen items with similar names.

We'll soon dive into more detail on all of this and there's much more to learn in the chapters that follow—and of course, there are plenty of recipes! From everyday staples like tomato sauce and green beans to creative canned creations like pineapple-flavored zucchini and Mexican-style chicken soup, I hope this book not only gives you the confidence to can, but gets you excited about it as well!

Water bath canning and pressure canning are the only two approved methods for canning that exist today. You may have heard of some old-fashioned ways, like canning using the oven or dishwasher—or using aspirin. However, these alternative methods have passed out of favor with time for a reason: they are not reliably safe!

CHAPTER ONE

PRESSURE CANNING BASICS

HAVE YOU EVER WONDERED WHY PRESSURE CANNING WORKS? It's actually a simple concept, and, if you are a bit of a science geek like me, quite fascinating!

The goal of pressure canning is to expose food to a high temperature under a specific pressure for a specific period of time to destroy microorganisms that are harmful if eaten. Pressure canning allows food to be heated to 240°F—the temperature necessary to destroy these microorganisms, including the botulism bacteria.

Botulism is rightfully one of the biggest fears for those new to canning, or those who don't can. It is flavorless and odorless. Even worse, it cannot be destroyed by boiling or hot water bath canning, which only reaches 212°F regardless of how long you boil the food. Botulism thrives in low-acid foods, in moist environments, and in an anaerobic (no oxygen) environment. All these conditions are present inside an *improperly* processed jar of food. Luckily, proper pressure canning creates a higher-temperature environment and can eliminate the risk of botulism in hours.

The other big fear when it comes to pressure canning is the safety of the pressure canner itself. Through the rest of this chapter, we'll discuss pressure canners, common terms, essential equipment, and using the pressure canner for the first time. By the end of this chapter, your fear should be a thing of the past, replaced by excitement to try your first recipe!

Keeping your workspace clean is essential when canning.

COMMONSENSE PRESSURE CANNING

Canning is a method of food preservation that requires common sense. You can play around with ingredients, invent new recipes, and even make artistic labels that wow your friends, but *cleanliness* and *organization* are the keys to germ-free jars of food.

The most important rule for pressure canning is **keep the process clean and simple**. This means keeping the work area and equipment as clean as you possibly can. You should also avoid nonstandard jars and any clutter—such as jar decorations—until after the food is ready for the pantry. You want as tidy a workspace as possible, especially as you're just getting started. Following are other important things to consider when planning for canning:

* Start in the garden: grow what you like.

* Choose your ingredients wisely—freshest and ripest.

* Know the proper steps to canning.

* Prepare and pack the right way.

* Use reliable, tested recipes.

* Update your canning knowledge.

Let's look at each more closely.

START IN THE GARDEN

After cleanliness, my most important piece of advice as you begin your canning journey is to grow what you and your family love to eat. You may have a really tasty-sounding recipe for pickled beets, but if you're the only one in your family who enjoys beets, they probably shouldn't take up much space in the garden! It's helpful to make a list of ingredients you find yourself using most frequently in your cooking, or the recipes you always rely on. Break down the recipes into ingredients and see what you might be able to grow and can yourself.

Take my family: We love tomatoes—fresh from the garden or in sauce, it matters not. My family wants to eat a tomato-based recipe every few days, so it only makes sense that I stock up on tomatoes in every form. Quart jars fit about one pound of processed tomatoes, so it's easy for me to plan the quantity I need to grow or buy from a local farmer.

This past year, I asked my favorite farmer to grow 100 pounds of tomatoes for me to can. Sound like a lot? Not when you do the math for my crew. We use two quarts of canned tomatoes in one meal. My plan was to have enough tomatoes for one tomato dish per week for a year. (We eat more than that, but this makes sure we don't waste tomatoes either.) You can do the same with meat, side-dish vegetables, soups, and more. By storing what you grow or buying during the season, when winter comes, your family will enjoy those summer flavors, without the sticker shock of winter shopping in the produce section.

Once you have a list of ingredients you want to can, make a general plan. Don't let that scare you. Planning for your pantry simply means thinking about the kinds of foods you will find useful to "shop" from in your own cupboards. I know my family likes soups for lunches, so I make plenty of soup bases. They also eat as much canned chicken as I can put up. Why buy tuna when you can preserve your own fish?

Canning may be simple enough, but it is work. Careful consideration about what you will preserve will keep you inspired and satisfied all year.

Using fresh, local produce that your family loves is the best place to start with canning.

CHOOSE YOUR INGREDIENTS WISELY

Always start with the freshest and ripest ingredients you can. This means you should be prepared to can before you shop. Even if you don't have the specific recipe ready to go, you can have all the equipment—jars, lids, rings, jar lifter, funnel, etc.—ready before you start. At a minimum, take inventory so if you're out of something, like jars or lids, you can pick them up when you go shopping.

It might be tempting to can less-than-perfect produce. Sure, canning "ugly" vegetables is okay. Sometimes you'll find tomatoes, carrots, or other vegetables that taste great but have an odd shape or other imperfection. These are fine for canning! However, *avoid canning wilted, soft, or bruised foods.* Starting with bruised or damaged food can give decay and bad bacteria that come with it a head start. Softer vegetables will also be even softer after canning, which most often works against your recipe. Use only firm, ripe foods at their peak of freshness.

KNOW THE STEPS TO CANNING

Successful canning means getting food quickly from the market or garden into jars. We'll cover the basic steps on page 27 and you should be familiar with them and your recipe *before* you start your work. The

Cutting uniformly sized pieces is key to ensuring the food in the jars cooks evenly.

middle of a recipe isn't the time to look something up. Even now, at the beginning of a season, I do a dry run through the process, pretending to can. It may look silly, but many times I realize I don't have a funnel or enough towels. My canning kitchen looks quite different from my regular kitchen; many items on my counters are put away and I have clear access around the room.

PREPARE AND PACK THE RIGHT WAY

Even the most pristine fruits and vegetables require preparation for canning. For one, you'll want to wash off any dirt—or scrub, in the case of root vegetables. You'll also remove stems, leaves, and any part of the plant you don't want to eat (such as a tough end of a rhubarb stalk).

Beyond cleaning and cutting, you'll also be following a recipe to cold pack or hot pack your produce. Cold packing, also known as raw packing, is exactly what it sounds like: packing raw vegetables or fruit in the hot jars and pouring hot liquid over top before canning. Hot packing, on the other hand, will have you cooking your vegetables or fruit before adding them—and often the cooking liquid—to the jars. If this seems overwhelming, don't worry; your recipe will always be your guide on whether to cold or hot pack the jars.

USE RELIABLE, TESTED RECIPES

This can be a sensitive topic. Many cooks have emotional ties to recipes—and their historical significance—especially when it comes to something as classic as canning. The conflict comes from techniques or recipes that have since been proven unsafe. This is one area where caution rules. If you have an heirloom recipe, you can certainly find an updated version of it from a reliable source. You may also be able to troubleshoot the unsafe issue—say, by increasing the time of cooking to match modern standards. When all else fails, can the jars based on the most delicate ingredient. So, if you were to can your Great-Auntie M's famous chicken soup, use the most modern techniques for canning chicken soup you can find, and can it in a pressure cooker under the correct pressure for that ingredient.

As much as I am a scratch cook who doesn't always stick to a recipe, when it comes to canning foods, following the rules is the only way. Changing things such as seasonings and how sweet you make the sugar syrup (see page 114) is fine, but be certain to follow canning recipes carefully and **do not experiment with time and temperature.**

UPDATE YOUR CANNING KNOWLEDGE

Each year I review the USDA's online guidelines for safe canning techniques. While my grandmother certainly knew what she was doing, I do things a little differently, and the next generation of canners will, too. We continue to learn ways to improve techniques, safety, and recipes as the years go by. It's always a good idea to keep abreast of best practices. Recipes and techniques are often handed down through families, and it can be hard to change or give something up, but remember safety is key.

In this book, we'll be referencing the most current USDA guidelines at the time of writing in 2017. While there may be further updates or minor adjustments if a new style of pressure cooker is introduced, these guidelines will serve you well overall no matter the year.

EQUIPMENT

When I started canning, I was a purist. I wanted to pretend my grandmother was a homesteader and she was teaching me her ways in the kitchen. I wanted to use only equipment she would have used—and everything needed to have a history. Soon, though, the reality was I needed to can large quantities to feed my growing family. There just weren't enough hours in the day to hand-shred 50 pounds of zucchini!

As I started using my food processor, a professional-quality chef's knife, and recipes with precise measurements and clear instructions, my canning became more efficient—and productive. I still have some of my old-fashioned equipment, but it has found a new home—lovingly displayed on the top of my cupboards!

That said, the equipment needed for canning is not extensive and it is affordable. If you're an avid home cook, you may already own much of what you need except, perhaps, the canner itself. Other than the canner, jars, and lids, most items on the following pages are recommended for your convenience.

PRESSURE CANNER

A pressure canner is, essentially, a heavy kettle designed to withstand higher pressure than a normal pot. While models vary in their features, all pressure canners offer a few common elements. For a quick reference, see the photo on page 16. For a more detailed explanation, read on!

A lid with a gasket will twist or clamp to fasten, removing the need for wing nuts.

COMMON CANNING TERMS

These terms are used throughout this book and the canning world. Once you understand the terminology, canning becomes a breeze.

Altitude: The elevation above sea level.

Blanch: Submerging food under boiling water for a few minutes, to loosen the skin or to stop enzymatic action in it. After blanching, the food is often placed in ice-cold water to stop the blanching process.

Boil: To heat liquid to 212°F, when bubbles break the surface.

Botulism: Food poisoning caused by ingesting the spores of *Clostridium botulinum*. The spores need an anaerobic environment (no oxygen) to survive. Botulism can be fatal.

Brine: A salt and water mixture used when pickling foods.

Canning salt: Salt that contains no iodine or noncaking agents. It is the salt used in most canning recipes.

Chutney: A thick recipe of sweet fruits and savory vegetables cooked with spices and vinegars.

Clear Jel: A modified food starch that will not break down when heated to a high temperature. It is a common thickener for canning foods.

Cold pack (or raw pack): Raw food placed in jars to be canned.

Headspace: The distance between the top of the food and the top of the mouth of the canning jar. Each canning recipe has a specified headspace.

High acid: High acid refers to a food's pH of 4.6 or lower. High-acid foods include most fruits and pickled foods. Most of these foods do *not* need to be canned in a pressure canner.

Hot pack: Hot pack is the method of heating food in hot liquid before placing it into jars.

Low acid: Foods with a pH higher than 4.6. Low-acid foods *must* be pressure canned.

Mason jar: A glass jar designed for heating foods and liquids. Mason jars can withstand the high pressure of a canner and should not be substituted with other food jars.

Oxidation: The reaction that occurs when cut fruits and vegetables are exposed to the air, such as apples turning brown.

Processing: The length of time necessary for canned food to remain in the pressure cooker to be completely heated throughout.

Purée: Food blended to a smooth, even consistency.

Saucepan: A heavy pot with a broad flat bottom and deep sides. Saucepans come in many sizes.

Screw band: A metal band with threads, used to attach the canning lid to the jar.

Simmer: To heat a liquid until numerous tiny bubbles rise to the surface.

Sterilize: To kill all microorganisms.

Before we get into the nuts and bolts (for some models, I mean that literally!), know this: a pressure cooker is not the same as a pressure canner. Yes, both devices use pressure and they look similar. However, pressure cookers are not designed for canning. Most models aren't large enough for cans and they don't have pressure gauges.

Pressure canners come in a wide range of models and sizes. When choosing the right model for you, consider how much you'll be canning at one time; for most people, a pressure canner in the 16- to 22-quart range will do the trick. The other main differences will be the gauge type (dial versus weighted) and cover type (metal-to-metal or lock-on with gasket). Let's get to it.

Locking cover: All pressure canners have a locking cover that can be closed in only one correct position. There are canners with covers that lock on with a rubber gasket between the cover and kettle, and other canners that have individual locking wing nuts around the edge. I have both styles and still use them both every year. Neither one is better, objectively, but I find I reach for the model with the gasket and lock-on cover more often.

I do this because the locking process for the pots is different and I prefer the locking procedure on the cover with the gasket. Unlike a metal-to-metal cover, which requires manual tightening, lock-on covers with gaskets have a specific closing procedure with matching markings for the lid and pot and/or clamps. This means there's either a "locked" or "not locked" situation, and no guessing as to the tightness of wing nuts. (Is this tight enough? Did I overtighten?)

No matter which lid type you have, always follow the manufacturer's instructions for locking the lid. Also, note that if your lid has a gasket, you'll need to clean it according to your manufacturer's instructions and use care. For example, some models may tell you to lubricate gaskets with cooking oil while others do not. Any damage to a gasket can affect the machine's ability to hold pressure correctly. Regularly inspect your gasket and replace at the first sign of wear.

Pressure gauge: Another feature that all pressure canners share is a gauge that displays the pressure inside the canner. There are two types of gauges and both work equally well. The first type of gauge is a weighted gauge. This gauge has no dial face, but instead has numbers engraved around its edges. This gauge will rattle when the correct pressure is reached; then it will rattle faster and allow some steam to escape if the pressure gets higher than necessary. Note that it's not better to have slow or fast jiggling with this type of pressure gauge.

PRESSURE GAUGE

RELEASE VALVE AND
OVERPRESSURE PLUG

LOCKING COVER

The fact that it is moving means it is maintaining the recommended pressure. In my opinion, this gauge is more foolproof as it requires less heat adjustment than a dial gauge.

The second type, a dial gauge, is an easy-to-read, clock face–style gauge. It has a hand that moves as the pressure increases. You adjust the heat while you watch the gauge. Start the timer once the canner gauge reaches the correct pressure and adjust the heat level with the goal of keeping the pressure gauge at the correct number for the period of time specified in the recipe.

As mentioned elsewhere, it's important to check your gauge for accuracy at least annually. The start of a new canning season is a great time to do this. Your county's cooperative extension office should be able to help and some manufacturers offer this service as well.

Release valve and overpressure plug: On the cover of your pressure canner, there is a release valve, which can also be referred to as a vent tube, petcock, or pipe vent in the manufacturer's manual. This release valve needs to be checked at the start of each canning session. Simply hold the cover up and make sure you can see light through the vent tube. If not, clean it with a pipe cleaner or however the manufacturer recommends. Note that this valve is where steam will come out and there are models where the weighted gauge will be on the valve.

Your pressure canner will also have an overpressure plug or safety fuse. This is a simple release that functions as a backup to the primary release valve/vent tube. The overpressure plug opens if the pressure gets too high due to the release valve being blocked. It is a safety feature not present on old-style pressure canners and you should not use a pot that's so old it does not have this important feature. This backup release mechanism is there for your safety. You should also look for the Underwriter's Laboratory (UL) seal to ensure the device's safety.

The manufacturer of your pot may have recommendations for keeping the release valve and overpressure plug clean and operational. Always follow the best practice directions for your pot.

Canning rack: Finally, your pressure canner will come with a rack. The rack will look like a circular dish with holes in it and it's designed to sit on the bottom of the canner. Jars will sit on top of the rack; its design allows for the circulation of steam around the jars. It also helps stabilize your jars so they don't knock together or against the sides of the canner (possibly breaking them). If your canner did not come with a rack or your rack breaks, you need to buy a new one. The best place to start is the canner's manufacturer. *Don't can without a rack.*

Weighted gauge models do not self-correct for altitude adjustments. This means at altitudes above sea level (higher than 1,000 feet), the pressure you set should be adjusted upward. See the guidelines on page 29.

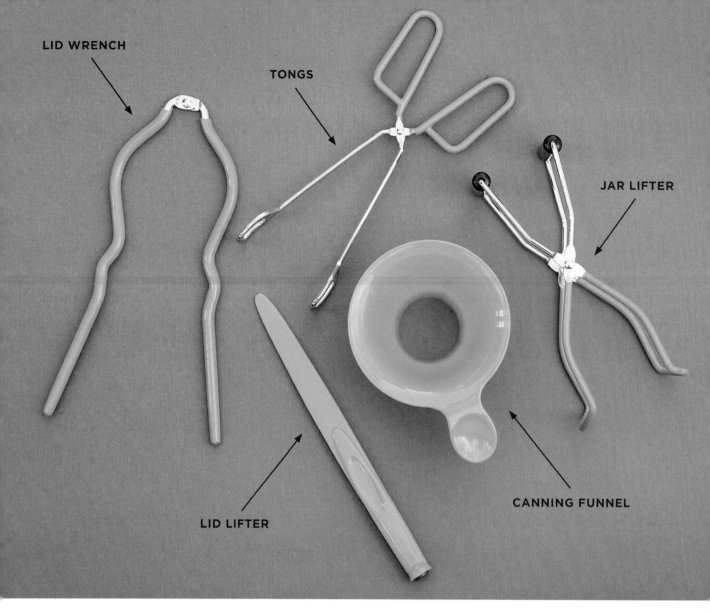

LID WRENCH

TONGS

JAR LIFTER

LID LIFTER

CANNING FUNNEL

Ball or Kerr jars (*right*) with 2-piece lids are the best option for beginners.

OTHER ESSENTIAL EQUIPMENT

Jars: These come in a variety of sizes and your recipe will indicate the correct size for the food you are canning. Jars are typically sold by the dozen for the most common jar sizes, though higher-end, fancier jars may be sold individually. For more information on jars, see page 24.

Jar lids: The lid is critical to a well-sealed jar, not just for the covering you can see it provides but also for the seal it creates underneath. The most common type of canning jars and lids are the variety made by large manufacturers such as Ball. The lids have two pieces: the flat lid itself and a screw band that goes around the outside of the lid (see the next item in this list). If you look at the underside of one of these canning jar lids, you will see a reddish-brown ring around the edge. This ring softens during processing and forms an airtight seal as it cools. Jar lids with this sealing compound are *not* reusable; however, you can reuse the jars and screw bands. Just buy a new pack of lids before the next canning session.

Screw bands: These bands are designed to hold the lid in place during processing. Since they can be reused, carefully inspect them for nicks, rust, and other signs the band has been weakened. As you'll read repeatedly in the recipes, the bands are screwed onto the jars until hand-tight and no tighter. They need to be loose enough to allow the jar lid to release air during processing. Screw bands can be removed after the jars cool completely to room temperature. Removing the band does not affect the lid seal and with no band to hide the seal it is easier to watch for any signs of leakage while the jar is in storage.

Canning funnel: Use a canning funnel to fill your jars. You might think this would be an optional piece of equipment; however, keeping the rim of the jar clean is very important. Because you will be working with very hot foods and liquids, using a funnel will help keep your hands from getting burned as well. A canning funnel has a wide mouth and is wider than a normal funnel at the bottom to accommodate big pieces of food. They are inexpensive, and I recommend buying a few. I have both metal and plastic funnels in my canning supplies and both work equally well.

Electronic scale: I recommend a digital scale that is reliable, and that includes a tare function. (Tare means you can place your container on the scale and then set it back to 0 before weighing your ingredients.) I also prefer battery-powered scales so you don't have to deal with a cord.

Jar lifter: This specialized item makes your canning experience much easier. You'll use the jar lifter to safely lift hot jars from the canner and protect your hands from hot water and steam. This tool has handles that stay cool, and the business end is rubber-dipped and curved to match the curvature of a jar. I have an old one and a newer model; the only difference is the newer one has plastic-covered handles and my older one has wooden handles. They both work equally well.

Wooden chopsticks (or a similar tool): When canning, there will be times when you need a long, straight object like a chopstick or the long handle of a wooden spoon. Really, you can use almost any (non-metal) object that can safely be poked into a jar to release trapped air bubbles and move food around as needed so it fits better. I like using chopsticks because they are cheap and effective. You can also use skewers, as long as they're wooden—you don't want to damage the glass jars. One other advantage or using chopsticks or skewers is you can use them in a pinch for other tasks, such as lifting bands out of hot water.

Lid lifter: Not to be confused with a jar lifter, this little tool is a must have. Once again, it comes into play when you're handling hot items— the best way to do anything at this stage is to do it safely. Your lids will be sitting in steaming-hot water and keeping them hot while they are being placed on jars is important. A lid lifter has a small magnet on the end that lifts the lid easily, allowing for an easy transfer to the jar. Before I owned one, I had to use tongs and it was often difficult to get the lids out of the water without burning myself at least a little. Save yourself from the same experience and buy a lid lifter.

Lid wrench: While the recipes in this book recommend hand-tightening lids before pressure canning, there are times when lids are tough to remove after canning. If you sometimes struggle with the lids on jars, this tool will make your life easier.

Dishtowels: I can't imagine canning without a clean stack of dishtowels for a variety of tasks. I use linen towels so there is no lint, but you can also use tightly woven cotton blends that have no nap. Just avoid fluffy towels that leave lint behind! Use your towels as a landing place for jars when removing them from the canner, for wiping jar rims before adding the lid, and for cleaning up spills as soon as they happen. I also use my dishtowels at various other times, to protect my hands from steam, for wiping off spoon handles if needed, etc. I start my canning session with at least 6 on the counter and usually end up using every one. I recommend white towels that don't look like your everyday towels, so you keep them just for canning and bleach them as needed.

Knives: I was taught a sharp knife is safer than a dull one and I have yet to find any evidence to the contrary. Canning involves a lot of food prep, and that means a lot of cutting. Sharp knives reduce hand fatigue and help you cleanly cut uniform pieces of food. You will not need a large number of knives; a paring knife and an 8- or 10-inch chef's knife will suffice. Keep them supersharp and learn how to cut properly with each if you don't already have strong knife skills. A little time spent learning will immediately pay you back in saved prep time.

Measuring cups: Plastic, metal, or glass, it doesn't matter which you choose as long as the markings are clear. What is important is having more than 1 set of measuring cups available. Having a second (or third) set at the ready will save you from stopping to clean in the middle of canning.

Measuring spoons: Just as with measuring cups, it's essential to have a spare set of spoons if you don't want to be caught unprepared while canning. Also, as much as I love the novelty of newer measuring spoons that slide or adjust to the measurement you need, I don't think they're as reliable for exact measurements—especially when measuring liquids. I stick to the easy-to-read, standard measuring spoons that have served cooks well for generations.

Rubber spatulas: While not necessary for every recipe, they are perfect for scraping out and moving sticky items such as jams and jellies. Rubber spatulas are easy to clean and they don't absorb flavors. They are also safer to use inside glass jars. I buy the type with a rubber end that can be removed from the handle for better washing and sanitizing.

Tongs: You probably have a pair of tongs in your kitchen already. They're perfect for handling hot food while keeping your hands far away—and that's true whether you're grilling or canning. I prefer the longer style that most people use for the grill, but shorter tongs will work as well.

Pot holders: Remember that even the thickest pot holder will allow steam through the fabric, so use them with caution. Having said that, pot holders are the tool of choice for moving hot, heavy pots around your stove. They can also insulate hot jars if you need to set one down on a cool countertop. Use a pot holder in a situation like this to avoid the possibility of cracking the glass jar or damaging your counter.

Ladles: A ladle should have a long handle and, although I love metal for many utensils, for ladles, plastic rules! Why? A ladle will spend quite a bit of time in boiling-hot foods when canning and a metal handle can conduct heat. The last thing you want is a ladle that's too hot to handle! I most often use a plastic ladle rated for high temperatures that measures ½ cup of liquid, and can double as a measuring device in a pinch.

Wooden spoons: Wooden spoons will not become soft or excessively bendable when submerged in hot liquid, unlike some cheaper plastic spoons. I use wooden spoons when cooking, and canning is no different. Actually, it just gives you the opportunity to use a wooden spoon even more—for example, you can use the handle for releasing trapped air bubbles.

NONESSENTIAL (BUT HELPFUL) EQUIPMENT

These items are not necessary for canning most recipes. However, some will make your life easier for every recipe and others are essential for a smaller group of recipes—such as jams and jellies.

Food processor: This is definitely not a "need it" item, but once you have one it is hard to go back. I use my food processor most often for shredding; it produces even results, and it greatly speeds up the job. I also use my food processor's slicing blade to cut thin slices for pickles. If you're on the fence about buying a food processor, borrow a friend's for a weekend. You will quickly see whether the speed and convenience are worth the cost (and cleanup).

Food mill: A food mill is designed to purée fruits and vegetables. It removes the seeds and skins as well. It's the surefire way to get silky smooth applesauce and the smooth consistency you crave in some recipes. Food mills were once hard to find, but now are sold in most big box stores. You also may get lucky and find a used model in good shape. While I don't recommend buying an old pressure canner, a used food mill is a different story. If cleaned well after every use and used carefully, this useful tool will last for many years.

Jelly bag: A jelly bag might sound like a very specialized tool, but it can be used for much more than just jelly. It is used to strain juice from fruits and vegetables after cooking. You transfer the produce to the bag and hang it over a pot or bowl so the juice can drip out and be collected. When making Tomato Ketchup (page 176), cooked tomatoes and other vegetables are cooked down and placed in a jelly bag. The excess tomato water drains away, leaving the thick pulp behind. The concentrated tomato pulp is the perfect base for thick, tasty ketchup. The tomato water can be discarded, or you could find a creative use— perhaps a new soup recipe!

Timer: Yes, you can use the timer on your stove for canning. However, having a dedicated timer you can slip in your pocket is handy. Find a timer you can hear easily, and one that can get splashed without damage. (This probably means buying one with a midrange price point.) I set my timer as soon as my pressure canner reaches the correct pressure, and slip it into my apron. If I get distracted (as much as I tell you not to, life does happen), I have a backup reminder that my jars are ready.

Labels: Labels are one item that may seem frivolous to beginners. After all, you can simply write the contents and date you preserved them on the metal lid. Yet labels have their place. Good labels adhere to the glass jars, making it simple enough to identify the contents and date without handling the jars to peek at the tops. Labels are also more attractive and, thus, are a nice touch if you're making the recipes as gifts—or if your cupboard is in view from your kitchen or dining room.

I use labels on my jars and try to change them each year. This means at a glance I know the quantity that is left from a given year—helpful especially on a shelf that has many of the same things, like tomatoes. With unique year-based labels, I know quickly that there are four more quarts to be used up before we start eating this year's supply. So labels are not critical to the canning process, but the more you can, the more you'll want to invest in at least simple labels.

LET'S TALK ABOUT JARS

Jars are about to become your new best friend. There are as many styles, sizes, shapes, colors, and uses for these sturdy glass containers as there are foods to put in them. Yet despite the fact that most jars have the same purpose (food preservation), not all jars are created equal.

The canning jars I recommend are the modern-style canning jars made by Ball and similar manufacturers. They are distinguished by their sturdy glass, clearly marked volumes, and 2-piece lids.

The main alternative to this style of jar is experiencing a resurgence, though more as a dry storage jar than for canning. This alternate style of jar, called a bail-type jar, made famous by Weck has two glass pieces—the jar and the lid—that are sealed together using a rubber gasket. Metal clips or a wire were used in conjunction to hold the lid on while canning, but the rubber seal acts like the modern seal under the lid to create the airtight environment you need to can.

*While this type of jar may be used for canning, I tend to recommend it for **refrigerated or dry storage** instead. Weck jars with brand-new rubber seals may be used if you follow the manufacturer's instructions, but they tend to fail the beginning canner more often. Even worse, similar-looking vintage jars may not be intended for pressure canning at all. If you collect glass jars to reuse for food storage like I do, keep them in rotation only for dry goods.*

So, what other options do you have within the recommended type of jars? You have a variety of sizes to choose from. The recipes in this book all come with a recommended jar size. Other considerations include the size of your canner, which may not accommodate the largest jars.

The other important consideration is the size of the jar's mouth opening. Canning jars commonly come with two options:

1. Regular-mouth jars have a small opening, about 2⅜ inches, but are good for liquids such as stocks or juices, and brothy soups. While many canners use only regular-mouth jars and have no trouble, keep

in mind that regular-mouth jars are a little harder to clean if there is residue inside.

Keep the opening size of the jar in mind when shopping for new jars.

2. Wide-mouth jars are my personal favorite for a few reasons. You can easily get a utensil inside to scrape them clean. I also like wide-mouth jars because, with their opening at about 3 inches, the jars are easier to fill for recipes with larger pieces. If your recipe will retain a firm texture, it's easier to remove the vegetables when serving as well.

There are many canning jar sizes, from half pints all the way up to gallons (these large jars are not usually used by home canners). With even grocery stores selling canning jars these days, you can easily find the right jar for the job. The recipes in this book, and elsewhere, recommend a specific size. For safety reasons, use the recommended size and don't switch up sizes unless there is a corresponding recommendation for canning. Let's look at some of the jars you'll use!

* **Jelly jar:** Not just for jellies and jams, these jars come in a range of sizes from 4 ounces to 12 ounces. They are the perfect size for gifting, and for the little condiments you want on the table, without

Jars also come in larger half-gallon or gallon sizes, but they are beyond the scope of the home canner. I use these supersize jars for dry food storage only.

having to eat from the container for an extended period of time. Can you imagine a quart of mustard, for example? Use jelly jars for mustards, ketchups, barbecue sauce, and small-batch recipes.

Jelly jars can also highlight a particular food. Jelly jars have wide openings so you can get out every last bite, and they are easy to clean. Due to their size, they require less processing time, which can be an advantage come canning day.

* **Half pint:** The half-pint jar gets quite a bit of mileage in my kitchen. When it comes to volume, these jars hold 8 ounces of food—and they also have the benefit of a wide mouth. I think it's the perfect size jar for relishes, pickles, and chunky chutneys. I use them exclusively for foods I want to use up quickly.

* **Pint:** Pint jars hold 16 ounces and can be used for many items. I use pints for soups I want to package as single lunches, salsas, and specialty recipes like cocktail onions. Pints are a manageable size for most recipes unless you are canning for a large family.

* **Quart:** Speaking of canning for the whole family, quart jars are my biggest workhorse. Quarts hold 2 pints, so you can package double the soup, sauce, etc. I always use quarts to can tomatoes, family-size recipes of sides like baked beans, and soups and broths meant to serve more at once. If you are canning sweet fruits, you may want to consider quart jars. It all depends on how fast your family goes through the food—in my house, the sweets go fast!

CARING FOR YOUR CANNING GEAR

Your pressure canner is a sturdy piece of equipment with simple parts. It does require some care, however. Before the canning season, inspect your canner and all the parts for any nicks or cracks. Check the cover and make sure the overpressure plug moves freely and the vent tube is unblocked. If your pressure canner has a rubber gasket, make sure it is pliable and clean.

Every year, the dial gauge on your pressure canner should be checked for accuracy. This is usually a free or inexpensive service that can be done at your local county extension office or hardware store. Do this early, as many services require that you drop off your equipment. If you wait until the last minute, you may have to wait for the return and miss a week or two of prime produce.

Between canning sessions, a quick rinse and dry of the pot is all that is needed before storage as long as you keep it clean as a matter of course. I keep my canner in the original box once it is clean and dry. That helps keep it from gathering dust and ensures it doesn't get dinged up. It also protects the gauge from damage.

When it comes to your canning jars, they are sturdy but, at the end of the day, they are glass. Run your hand gently over the rim of each jar the day before you want to use it to find any small nicks. Also, hold each jar up to the light and look at the glass. You will be able to see small cracks if there are any.

Chips, nicks, and cracks are all signs the glass is no longer fit for canning. It is for this reason I never recommend letting your family use canning jars as drinking glasses. Something that seems as harmless as the teaspoon you stir your sweet tea with can weaken the glass. If you love the look of canning jars, buy a set just for drinking and keep the ones you use for canning stored separately.

The screw bands are the backbone of a good seal. When you purchase a box of canning jars, they come with the lid and band on each jar. The lids are not reusable, but the bands are. Once your jars cool, carefully remove the screw band and store the sealed jar. Screw bands can be reused until they become bent or corroded. Wash and dry your bands before storing them and plan to replace a few each year. I recommend keeping a box on hand for this purpose.

Likewise, keep measuring cups and spoons in good shape by keeping them clean. I like to keep all my canning supplies in the same drawer and I like to sanitize my supplies before each canning session (see sidebar, page 28). This ensures my surfaces and items are as clean as possible before I start. Using plastic items means they can be sanitized without the risk of corrosion.

Every canning season should start with a visual inspection. This includes removing the lid and checking the gasket for some models.

THE PRESSURE CANNING PROCESS

No matter what food you are preserving, it requires the same steps to pressure can.

* If you're using an electric pressure canner, you will need to rely on additional instructions from the manufacturer to achieve the desired pressure for the appropriate length of time—you will not adjust it with a stovetop burner like the other models.

* Likewise, if you're using a weighted-gauge model, consult the manufacturer's instructions on setting the canning pressure and for information on how to evaluate whether the canner is maintaining pressure.

CLEAN IS BEST

We all have clutter in our kitchens. As much as *things* make our house our home, they also collect dust and dirt.

When you are canning, clear your kitchen counters completely of anything you aren't using for the canning process. I remove all my small appliances, jars of utensils, and my extra measuring cups and storage containers. If I am not going to touch the item for canning, it gets removed.

This may seem like extra work, but it ensures the work area can be cleaned thoroughly. It also means you won't accidentally knock into something and ruin some of your hard work. If you're wondering where to put everything, do what I do: Make your kitchen table a temporary countertop! Sure, it clutters up the kitchen table, but that's okay. You won't be using it while you can.

CLEANING

Okay, is your counter free of all clutter? Great! Now it's time to wipe down all the surfaces with hot, soapy water to remove any grease and dirt. This is the cleaning step; it will remove any small particles of food or other impurities from your countertop. Only once your counter and work surfaces are clean are you ready to move on to sanitizing.

SANITIZING

To sanitize, you can use a commercial product, such as Star San. However, most people prefer to use what they have on hand: bleach. Create a sanitizing mixture by mixing 1 tablespoon food-safe bleach with 1 gallon water. This concentration of bleach in water, 200 ppm, doesn't need to be rinsed off but it does need to air-dry before the surface is considered sanitized. Do what I do and pour the mixture in a spray bottle. Once you've cleaned your counter, mist it with the sanitizing solution, and wipe so you have a thin layer across the surface. Let it air-dry and you're ready to move on to canning!

The USDA specifically calls out a serious error that can cause unsafe canning:

As mentioned previously, the **internal canning temperature drops at high altitudes**. To correct for this, adjust the pressure of your canner upward if you live above sea level. USDA guidelines recommend increases as follows for **dial gauge canners**. The recipes in this book specify dial gauge pressure for canners below 2,000 feet.

For recipes at 11 pounds:

2,001 to 3,000 feet ....11½ pounds
3,001 to 4,000 feet ....12 pounds
4,001 to 5,000 feet ....12½ pounds
5,001 to 6,000 feet ....13 pounds
6,001 to 7,000 feet...............................13½ pounds
7,001 to 8,000 feet ....14 pounds
8,001 to 9,000 feet ....14½ pounds
9,001 to 10,000 feet ....15 pounds

For recipes at 6 pounds:

2,001 to 4,000 feet ....7 pounds
4,001 to 6,000 feet ....8 pounds
6,001 to 8,000 feet ....9 pounds
8,001 to 10,000 feet ....10 pounds

For **weighted gauge canners**, as soon as you get over 1,000 feet in elevation, you should switch from the 5-pound to the 10-pound or the 10-pound to the 15-pound setting for safety, depending on the recipe. The recipes in this book specify pressure for weighted gauge canners below 1,000 feet.

If **air is trapped in your canner**, it lowers the temperature obtained at any pressure. Take care to avoid this.

Here is a quick review of the steps we'll take:

1. Prepare the canning area.
2. Prepare the canning jars and utensils.
3. Prepare the canner.
4. Prepare the food.
5. Fill the jars to the correct level.
6. Fill the canner.
7. Follow the recipe instructions.
8. Cool the jars.
9. Check the seals; label and store the jars.

(A)

PREPARE THE CANNING AREA

If you skipped the last few pages (go back and read them!), preparing the area means removing whatever you don't need to pressure can from the counter: extra utensils, small appliances, daily dishes, and other items should be placed elsewhere while you focus on canning. Clean and sanitize your countertops and anything else you think will come in contact with the canning jars and lids before they go into the canner (see page 28). (A)

PREPARE THE CANNING JARS AND UTENSILS

The jars and utensils you will use should be examined beforehand to make sure nothing is chipped or broken. The jars and utensils you will use should be washed in hot, soapy water before use. The clean jars should then be placed in hot—not boiling—water. Single-use lids need to be clean. It is no longer necessary to heat Ball or Kerr brand lids, but if you choose to heat them, do not boil them.

One tip for being ready to can is to place your jars in the dishwasher and run it through a sanitizing cycle. You can leave your jars in the dishwasher until you actually need to use them. I often do this the night before so they are waiting for me first thing in the morning. Before I had a dishwasher, I would wash them the night before and place them on linen hand towels on the sideboard. In the morning, all I had to do was place them in hot water to heat while I prepped my food.

PREPARE THE CANNER

Follow the manufacturer's guidelines for filling your specific canner. You'll likely need to insert the canning rack, add 2 to 3 inches of water to the bottom of the canner, and get that water preheated.

PREPARE THE FOOD

Your recipe may require a variety of preparation techniques before you can it. Fruits or vegetables must be washed, and perhaps peeled, and cut according to the recipe guidelines. Some foods are also browned or otherwise precooked. When making broth or soup, you may cook the entire recipe before you can. In any case, your recipe will clearly provide these directions.

FILL THE JARS TO THE CORRECT LEVEL

Once your food is ready to can, the sanitized jars must be filled to the recipe's specifications. (B) Nearly all recipes in this book provide cooking liquid or heated water to top up your jars to the proper fill level. Note that all recipes require some amount of headspace, the room between the top of the food or liquid and the rim of the jar. (Proper headspace allows the food to expand and air to be forced out during the canning process.) Once the jars are full, use a nonmetallic tool to remove any air bubbles. (C) Wipe the rims with a clean damp cloth, (D) carefully place the lids on, (E) and hand-tighten the screw bands around the lids. (F)

FILL THE CANNER

Gently place your jars in the canner on top of the canning rack, making sure they do not touch (using a jar lifter, grab the jars below the screw band). (G) When the canner is full, double check that all jars are upright and not tilted. Place the lid on the canner and lock it according to the manufacturer's instructions.

If you accidentally prepared more food than will fit in your pressure canner, do not pack jars for the next batch and let them sit. Instead, I recommend repeating the steps here in the same order: prepare the food, prepare the canner, pack the jars, and then fill the canner once again.

Follow your manufacturer's guidelines to close and lock the pressure canner. If you're using a model with more manual controls, you typically need to secure the lid, open the petcock (vent pipe) or leave the weight off the vent port, and place the pot over high heat until steam flows continuously for about 10 minutes. (H) At this point, it is time to close the petcock or vent port and let the canner pressurize—it should take less than 5 minutes. (I) Again, always follow your machine's instructions as you must close and lock the lid properly to maintain pressure!

(F)

FOLLOW THE RECIPE

With your lid locked in place, use your canner's settings or a stovetop burner to get a steady stream of steam from your pressure canner for 10 minutes or according to the manufacturer's guidelines. *Only once you do this should you close the vent and start bringing the canner to the proper pressure.*

For an electric pressure canner or a weighted-gauge model, you will most likely be instructed to set the pressure now. If you're using the stovetop to supply the heat, keep the pot at a temperature that maintains the pressure at or above the recommended level for the duration of the recipe's recommended processing time.

No matter which type of pressure canner you use, *start timing your recipe once the pressure on the dial gauge is correct or when the weighted gauge moves* as described by the manufacturer. In other words, if your recipe says the pressure should be held at 11 pounds for 30 minutes, start the timer only once the pot reaches 11 pounds, not when you first apply the heat.

Pressure Dip?

Did your pressure dip below the recipe's recommended pressure? *The only safe way to remedy this is to bring the pot back to the recommended pressure and restart the timer.* **Never** let the timer continue once a pot falls below the recommended pressure amount as you can no longer guarantee the safety of the canned food.

Use care not to create large drops or increases in pressure, even above the recommended range, as this could prevent some of the jars from sealing properly. (Again, if you're using a weighted gauge, the manufacturer will provide instructions on how to monitor the pressure.)

COOL THE JARS

Once your recipe is finished cooking, turn off the heat. After some of the cooling time has passed, you can safely remove the lid. The amount of time it takes before you can safely release pressure and remove the lid varies by machine. It's often about 10 minutes after the machine reaches 0 pounds pressure.

Do not attempt to speed the cooling by putting your canner in the fridge or freezer, or by placing it in a sink full of cold water. The canner needs to cool without your assistance. Trying to cool the canner faster can result in unsafe canned foods, as well as imperfect seals. Once

the lid is off, do not remove the jars immediately; let them continue to cool inside the canner for about 20 minutes. This is a good time to set up a place for the jars to rest once you remove them. I recommend setting a clean towel in an out-of-the way place in the kitchen, away from people who may be tempted to touch the cooling canned food and away from any drafts. You may need a spot for the cans to rest for up to 24 hours as they cool, so choose wisely!

Once you're ready to remove the jars, use a jar lifter to remove them and place them on the clean dishtowel, about 1 inch apart. (J) Do not disturb the jars while they cool and do not try to remove the bands yet. You will hear the jars "ping" as each lid finishes sealing during the cooling process.

CHECK THE SEALS AND LABEL AND STORE THE JARS

Once the jars cool to room temperature, remove the screw bands and check that each jar is sealed properly: Press gently on the lid. It should be concave (dip inward) if you have a good seal. It should feel firm to the touch and it should not move or dip when you push on it. Do not tip or shake the jars, but do wipe off any residue that may have escaped during the time in the canner. Label your jars and place the sealed jars in a cool, dry location. If you have any jars that did not seal properly, refrigerate them and use them within a week or two (depending on the recipe).

BE PRESENT, SAFE, AND EFFICIENT

No matter what you are canning, the basic procedure is the same. Beginners will undoubtedly make a mistake here or there though, and even experienced canners can forget something. That's why when people ask me for my "secrets" for canning, I usually offer these three—my golden rules of canning.

BE PRESENT

Never have a canning session when you are tired or distracted. Don't can if you are enjoying a glass of wine or having friends over for good conversation. Canning is not difficult, but it does require precision and careful monitoring. Skipping a step or missing a drop in pressure can let bacteria slip by or keep a batch of jars from being sealed properly. Your minor distraction can cause major illness. At the very least, it will probably result in wasted food.

BE SAFE

Canning involves sharp knives, hot water, scalding-hot steam, and hot jars. Always cut carefully, move hot water and other burning-hot items around your work area safely, and plan for children and pets to play elsewhere while you can. Few other hobbies require high heat as essential to success—even the food you can will be heated to above boiling temperatures. Always make sure you have a place for the hot jars on the counter before you need to transfer them and make double sure that place is far away from a place children could be tempted to touch.

BE EFFICIENT

This third rule helps you follow the first two rules: be efficient when canning. Keep only the items you need out in the open. Clear away all the tchotchkes and other homey decor. Clean work surfaces thoroughly and prepare enough food for one canner load at a time. Your jars and lids should be ready to go before you start so you can methodically go through the recipe steps and get the food into the jars in record time. It is important, no matter what type of cook you are the rest of the time, that you are a disciplined and efficient canner.

CHAPTER TWO

STORAGE, TROUBLESHOOTING, AND OTHER CONSIDERATIONS

NOW THAT YOU'VE READ THE FIRST CHAPTER, congratulations! You now know the basics of canning. Hopefully that also means you've purchased the equipment you need to can—maybe you even have a recipe or two under your belt.

But knowing how to can is just the beginning. Chances are you'll have ups and downs along the way. Maybe a jar or two didn't seal. Or maybe you have a cloudy jar and are wondering if it's safe to eat. (Alert: don't eat it!) This chapter covers some of the most common problems when canning, as well as how to spot unsafe food and jars.

This chapter also addresses a few other important issues, such as proper storage. After all, if you don't put up your canned goods with as much care as you can them, they won't last as long or taste as fresh when you open them.

AFTER YOU CAN

Let's start this chapter where we ended the last one—at the end of a canning session. As you already know, the last step is removing the bands from your canning jars and checking the seals by examining the tops (which should be concave). Then it's on to wiping down the jars and labeling them for storage.

While you might be tired after an afternoon of canning, do not skip these important steps. It's easy to think "I'll do it later" when it comes to labeling. But I've found it's best to label the foods with the recipe name and date immediately after you finish canning when the information is fresh in my mind, and before I forget to do it.

As you get started in canning, it's also important to keep a notebook. Jot down your notes while the day is fresh in your mind. Did one jar fail to seal? Did you have any issues maintaining pressure? How long did it take for the pot to reach pressure? These notes are the beginning of your foundation of canning knowledge. Without detailed notes, it will take you much longer to develop your skills and master your own canning setup.

So, what's next? Clean jars should be stored upright, in neat rows, in a cool, dark place. You don't want the jars exposed to light, nor do you want them exposed to temperatures that fluctuate. In other words, while an outdoor shed or garage might be cool, dark, and the temperature never goes above 60°F in the winter, it might fluctuate by 20°F to 30°F some days or throughout a season. This is not an ideal environment for canned goods. Store them indoors in a pantry. Neat rows are essential so you can easily see that each jar looks the same as it did the day it was placed on the shelf. It's easier to spot a jar that looks different from the rest when they're aligned in a neat row.

If you find a white residue on your jars as you go to store them, don't panic. If it disappears when you wipe the jar but comes back when it dries, this is just a sign that your water has a high mineral content. Wiping it with a cloth dampened in a vinegar-water mixture will remove it.

As far as what to avoid when storing your jars, here are a few common mistakes to be aware of:

1. Do not tip and shake your jars from time to time to keep them evenly mixed. Let them settle and *only stir them after opening.*

2. Do not place jars with no labels on the shelf. Add the name of the food and date it was canned to each jar. If you're in a hurry, at least write that information on the lid with a marker!

3. Keep jars out of direct sunlight. If your pantry's light changes from season to season, double check to make sure there isn't a jar or two getting light for a couple hours a day.

4. Do not stack jars. This can keep you from seeing if a lid has loosened or become unsealed. If you need to fit more in the pantry, adjust your shelf height or install more shelves instead.

5. If you find an unsealed jar, do not try to save the food by reheating it. Your health is not worth a jar of food.

USE WHAT YOU CAN

If you enjoy cooking (and you probably do since you are reading this book), you will enjoy having shelves of canned goods based on your tastes and needs. When your basic foods are customized to your taste and ready at your fingertips, you can conveniently "shop" in your own store at home—with better quality and flavor than the grocery store. If you start planning meals to include at least one ingredient of your own, you will come to rely on your handiwork and see how that work is well worth the effort.

We have all seen beautiful photos of pantries bursting with rainbows of jars from floor to ceiling. I only wish my pantry was that colorful and full! The truth is, I can what my family will actually eat, and I run out of room before I run out of ideas.

I once wrote down the recipes my family uses the most. It was easy to see we eat mostly from scratch, but generally only used about two dozen or so recipes year-round with any regularity. Doing the same for your household will help you get a handle on what canned foods you'd use the most.

Make a simple spreadsheet listing your favorite recipes, with the ingredients you need, and identify the ingredients you could can. Of course, canning also depends on your access to certain fruits and vegetables. If you grow your own, the success of your garden may drive how much you can (unfortunately, I know this issue well). However, if you have access to a farmers' market, you can usually find whatever quantity you need to round out your own harvest.

Consider what your family likes to eat when selecting your canning recipes.

You should also consider common serving sizes at your house. If you are a canning for just one or two people, it makes more sense to preserve your foods in pints and half pints. A simple way to think about this is by looking at a can of vegetables from the grocery shelf. Do you use one can of beans when preparing a meal? If so, you can safely can a pint or half pint of beans. For my family, I found we use a pint of beans, relish, or corn, but need a larger amount—a quart—for applesauce or pickles. (Yes, my family eats a pint of zucchini relish at a meal and would eat even more if I would give it to them!)

3 REASONS TO EAT FROM YOUR PANTRY

1. Can for inspiration. I often go to the pantry, find a canned vegetable that catches my eye, and use that ingredient as a starting point for dinner. Alternatively, try the same exercise as forced inspiration: If you have way too many canned carrots beckoning, look for new recipes that will use up those carrots!

2. Can for every day and for rainy days. When I began canning, it was sometimes difficult to break out a jar I had worked so hard creating. You may find you hoard some of your more precious jars or favorite recipes. A great way around this is to compromise with yourself. If you find you have a favorite you're reluctant to use, save yourself just a jar or two for a special treat. This will let you work through the rest and ensure you don't end up with expired food, while also guaranteeing you have a jar or two of something special come February.

3. Can to save money. Utilize your pantry foods to save money. Were you about to run to the store because you have "nothing" on hand for dinner? What about all those canned tomatoes? Be resourceful about dinner, using mostly canned goods and grains you have on hand.

Always leave the headspace recommended in the recipe so the food and liquid have room to expand under pressure.

SPOTTING PROBLEMS IN THE PANTRY

No matter how hard you try, occasionally a jar will go off. When this happens, it is critical that you do *not* try to salvage the food. Knowing the signs of spoilage and how to care for your canned goods is an essential part of pressure canning. Let's take a look at some things you might find in the pantry.

Sealed jars that don't stay sealed. First of all, your jars have to seal or they don't make it onto the shelves. Period. That said, a jar can unseal over time. Check your jars regularly and, *if one becomes unsealed, discard it immediately.* If more than one seal fails from the same batch, go back to your notes from that canning day to try to figure what went wrong. You'll then know if that same thing happens again, you'll need to keep a very close eye on your jars.

Food fades in color. Over time, food can fade yet still be safe to eat. However, with that fading comes loss of nutrients. Fading food can occur due to exposure to light though. With exposure to sunlight also comes additional heat, which will decrease the shelf life of your food. Make sure you store food in a cool, dark place and use it within one year.

Foods that darken in color. If food floats to the top of the liquid in the jar, it may darken where it is exposed to air. This is not dangerous as the canning killed any harmful bacteria, but it is visually unappealing. It is important to cover the food with liquid before canning to try to avoid this; if you have food that breaks the surface of the liquid, you run the risk of darkened food.

Changes in food other than fading or darkening. Your food should not bubble, swell, shrivel, or become cloudy. If any of those things happens, discard the food. Bacteria can cause a variety of visible changes in your foods and it is never safe to try even a tiny taste if you see changes other than fading or darkening.

Mold in jars. *Mold is never safe* in your jars. You might see it grow on the contents of the jars, on the jar walls, or even on the underside of the lid. Do not try to remove the mold or think that heating it will help. Mold in jars is dangerous as it contains spores that become airborne when disturbed. When there is mold found in any can you should discard everything, including the jar and its contents.

TROUBLESHOOTING

Even the best canners occasionally have issues. However, there are some common issues and questions I get from beginning canners. From the mysterious disappearance of liquid to cracked jars, let's run through a few of the greatest hits.

WHERE DID ALL THE LIQUID GO?

When you remove your jars from the canner, sometimes there is not enough liquid left in the jars to cover the food. There are many potential reasons for this, but it's usually one of the most common causes to blame. Here are the top culprits for losing liquid during the canning process and tips on how to avoid them.

* **Jars that are too full or too tightly packed.** When food and liquid are boiled, they expand. If there is not enough headspace in the jar, liquid is forced out. Always follow the recipe guidelines for recommended headspace. More is not always better when it comes to canning!

* **Air bubbles are trapped in the canned food.** Trapped air bubbles can indicate the food was not canned properly. Always make sure to release air bubbles with a straight wooden or plastic utensil before topping up the jar to the specified level and sealing.

* **Pressure fluctuations.** If pressure fluctuates during processing, liquid may be forced out of the jars. Control the pressure carefully and avoid frequent adjustments. If you experience a quick increase or decrease in pressure—even above the recommended recipe guideline for minimum pressure—make sure to check your jars carefully once they cool.

* **Pressure is released too rapidly.** A rapid release of pressure can also cause liquid to be forced out of the jars. This is one reason you should always allow your canner to cool to room temperature on its own. Never try to help it along by placing it in the fridge, freezer, or a bath of cool water.

WHY DID MY JARS BREAK?

It has happened to everyone who cans: The excitement of opening the canner quickly turns to shock as you are greeted with a mess of broken jars and wasted food. Even just one jar breaking can put a damper on a fun day of canning. Here are some of the most common reasons glass breaks in the canner and tips to prevent this from happening to you.

* **Reusing store product jars** instead of home canning jars is a surefire way to get a broken jar—or three—on canning day. Even if canning lids and rings fit the commercial jars, the glass may not be made to be reheated under pressure. This is why I recommend only using actual canning jars for your home canning.

* If a jar has been **damaged prior to canning**, it's probably going to crack under pressure. Inspecting each jar before you use it, making sure it has no chips or cracks, is crucial. Hold the jar up to the light and take your time during the inspection. The smallest crack is all it takes for the jar to break in the canner.

* Related to this last point, jars can be **damaged by metal objects**. Using metal spoons and other metal utensils to rearrange foods or release air bubbles can nick and weaken the jar. Even a small amount of damage to a canning jar can cause breakage once it's under pressure. It's important you don't damage the jars you've already inspected on canning day.

* If you place **jars in the canner without a rack**, they will not be stable during the canning process and they can break. Always use a rack when canning.

* **Hot jars** can crack if they are placed on a cold surface. In addition to saving your countertops, placing jars that come out of the canner onto a clean dishtowel, away from drafts, will keep you from losing part of your batch due to breakage.

* When **hot jars are filled with cold water, or cold jars are filled with hot food**, the glass can crack. Avoid this by keeping jars hot and only filling hot jars with hot food.

WHAT ARE THE MOST COMMON CANNING MISTAKES (AND HOW DO I AVOID THEM)?

All cooks make mistakes, but canners need to be precise and careful with their canning technique. There are common mistakes that many canners make, which could be, at the least, wasteful and, at the most, dangerous. Let's take a look at what to avoid and why.

* **Using outdated canning methods.** This is, perhaps, one of the most important things to avoid when canning. Just because your grandparents did something and survived doesn't mean you should do it as well. There's a reason today's safety standards differ from the standards decades ago. We have learned a great deal about safe canning and there's no reason not to follow the current canning guidelines.

* **Overpacking jars.** Perhaps the most common mistake beginning canners make is not leaving adequate headspace in the canning jars. Every recipe has proper headspace requirements and this requirement is essential for safe canning. Filling the jars beyond the recommended level means the food won't have room to expand while under pressure. The pressure on overfilled jars forces liquid out between the lid and rim, and can keep the lid from sealing properly as the pressure returns to normal. Always fill jars leaving the correct amount of headspace.

* **Not adhering to proper pressure requirements and times.** While not following a recipe's instructions is not a common mistake canners make, some canners are not even aware when they are "breaking the rules." The length of time needed for the recipe is essential for heating the food to the center of the jar. If the pressure drops below the recommended level, it is not safe simply to resume the timer once you're back at pressures—yes, even if you were nearly done with a recipe! If the pressure drops below the recommended level, you must restart your timer to ensure safe canned food.

* **Interchanging ingredients in a recipe.** Recipes for pressure canning are designed with a length of cook time and pressure designed around the ingredients, both to properly heat them through and to take into account ingredient variables such as acidity. Do not change the recipe or you will risk your food being canned improperly, and spoilage can develop. The only changes you can make safely are to spices, such as oregano, thyme, etc.

* **Leaving screw bands on jars.** Leaving bands on jars can lead to stuck lids and can mask other issues—namely, it is hard to tell if the lid sealed properly if the edge of the seal is hidden by a band.

* **Starting with overripe foods.** Food that is pressure canned past its prime will result in recipes that have an unappealing color, texture, or flavor. If a food has started to decay, simply cutting out the visible "bad" spots may not be enough to remove all the decay. Your food must be as perfectly ripe as possible to get the best, and safest, results.

* **Overcooking recipes before canning.** Since foods are cooked at such high heat during the pressure canning process, if recipes are cooked too long before placing the food in the jars, the resulting food can become mushy. While there's no safety concern here, your family will have to eat their way through your mistake!

FINDING AND PREPARING FOOD FOR CANNING

The best canning results comes from the best ingredients. Logically, the first step toward making that perfect recipe is starting with perfectly ripe ingredients. In addition to ripeness, check your produce for excess bruises or other damage. A small spot is acceptable if it's surface damage, but you don't want to can anything that shows signs or deep damage or rot. Always err on the side of caution. If you've already bought the produce, save those less-than-perfect pieces for your day-to-day meals; reserve only the best for your jars.

I am also a believer in using locally grown produce. If you garden, growing your own fruits and vegetables for canning makes it certain to know there are no dangerous pesticides or other chemicals used to treat what you can. Local farmers' markets are the next best option. Get to know your local farmers. Even farms that don't pursue organic certification may abide by the organic rules—or even stricter standards. Talk to the farmers and see if you can visit their farms. Once you know who grows the best produce, make a point of checking in with them throughout the growing season. Getting a sense of what's available when—and at what price—will help you plan recipes for next year.

There are other reasons a good relationship with your farmer or farmers' market vendor pays off. If you tell them you're looking to can, they can bring you enough to make a batch of whatever you want. I often do this when I want to can large numbers of tomatoes. I set the date with my vendor and arrive at the farmers' market before it opens for business. They tend to appreciate this as well; otherwise,

you may buy all their tomatoes for the day and that risks angering other customers.

So, you've bought the best produce. Now what? Most foods require some basic preparation. You should thoroughly wash your produce, especially if you're not removing the skin. Your recipe will likely have you process the fruit or vegetables into pieces of a certain size; nearly every recipe requires uniform pieces. Similar-size pieces cook at the same rate, while pieces that vary too much in size may result in some being overcooked or some being undercooked. Some recipes also call for precooking the produce in a specific liquid; others simply use water with a bit of salt.

When it comes to meat and seafood, both require careful handling before you can them. While it should go without saying, you only want the best-quality meat and fish for canning—never can expired meat or fish! Generally, you keep meat and fish cold until the day of canning. Most recipes will instruct you to bring them to room temperature. While you can freeze meat and fish to extend their shelf life, do not do so if you are canning. Freezing results in an inferior texture for many recipes. It's not unsafe, as long as you follow the recipe, but, if you're doing the work to can, why not ensure the end result is as tasty as possible.

Finally, though it's been said before, never overpack a jar with anything you are canning. This overlaps with careful preparation as you need to use care for certain recipes to cut pieces to the right size. For example, if you cut carrot sticks too long, the tops may stick out of your canning liquid if you leave the proper headspace.

While you shouldn't use any past-prime or damaged produce, there is nothing wrong with canning "ugly" produce. Often farmers will have oddly shaped carrots, peppers, squash— even tomatoes—available at a discount due to their appearance. As long as they are ripe and show no signs of damage, they are a great find for canning!

A visit to the local farmers market often leads to a canning session!

CHAPTER THREE

CLASSIC VEGETABLE RECIPES

CANNED VEGETABLES CAN BE SO MUCH MORE than the shriveled peas served in the school cafeteria. Home-canned vegetables are bright, plump, and full of natural flavor—without all the added salt and preservatives you find in factory-processed varieties.

Canning pairs perfectly with another of my favorite hobbies—gardening. I know that no matter how much I grow, I can preserve it all for a later date. This justifies my seed and plant collection! Not a gardener? No problem. If you are lucky enough to have a well-stocked farmers' market in your area, get to know the farmers who sell there. Tell them you're planning to can some of what you buy and ask what they like to put up. If you become a regular, some farmers will begin setting aside new vegetables for you to try canning—you're sure to learn a new recipe or two.

Buying local is the best strategy for procuring ingredients whenever possible. These farmers pick their produce at its peak ripeness and bring it directly to market. They do not have to pick underripe fruits and vegetables and ship them thousands of miles, like traditional grocery store suppliers. You will have the best-quality food available in your area and you'll be supporting your local economy. As an added bonus, your local farmers' market is usually less expensive than the grocery store.

Because there are so many options for canning vegetables, I selected recipes for this chapter that are classics in my pantry. They are great introductions to the joy of canning.

STEWED TOMATOES

On a cold night on the farm, one of our favorite comfort foods is a simple meal of hot, stewed tomatoes and buttered noodles. We pan fry some extra onions and peppers to go with the onion and pepper in these tomatoes, but, otherwise, the jarred goodness carries the meal. I've found my family doesn't much notice the skin on the tomatoes once they've been canned, but if you want to remove the skins before canning it's easy enough. Simply dip the tomatoes in boiling water and immediately transfer them to an ice-water bath. The skins will peel off easily.

PROCESSING TIME: 15 MINUTES | PRESSURE: 10 POUNDS WEIGHTED GAUGE, 11 POUNDS DIAL GAUGE
YIELD: 4 PINTS

12 to 14 large tomatoes, quartered

½ cup roughly chopped onion

⅓ cup roughly chopped green bell pepper

2 teaspoons sugar

1 teaspoon canning salt

1. Prepare 4 pint jars and the canner: Clean the jars and prepare the 2-piece lids according to the manufacturer's guidelines. Keep the jars in hot but not boiling water until you're ready to use them. Prepare the canner by filling it with 2 to 3 inches of water and bringing it to a simmer, or according to your manufacturer's directions.

2. In a large pot over medium-high heat, combine the tomatoes, onion, and green bell pepper.

3. Add the sugar and salt, stirring to dissolve. Bring the mixture to a boil and reduce the heat to a simmer. Cook for 15 minutes, stirring often to prevent burning.

4. Carefully fill the jars with the hot tomato mixture, leaving ½ inch of headspace.

5. Remove any air bubbles with a plastic or wooden utensil, adding more tomatoes or liquid as needed to maintain the proper ½-inch headspace.

6. Wipe the rims and seal the jars hand-tight with the 2-piece lids.

7. Carefully transfer the filled jars to the rack inside the pressure canner. Process the jars at the pressure listed above for 15 minutes. (For complete canning instructions, see page 27.)

8. Let the canner return to 0 pounds pressure. Wait 10 minutes more, then carefully open the canner lid according to the manufacturer's instructions.

9. With a jar lifter, remove the jars and place them on a clean dishtowel away from any drafts. Once the jars cool to room temperature, check the seals. If any jars have not sealed, refrigerate them and use the tomatoes within 2 weeks. Label the remaining jars with the recipe name and date before storing.

THE SWEETEST CANNED CORN

If summer to you means biting into a fresh ear of corn, you should be canning corn for a taste of summer come fall or winter. Just a bite of this canned sweet corn will make your taste buds very happy. Warning: it may make you want to fire up the grill in December! If you use good-quality corn, it remains plump and slightly crisp through the canning process. The secret to great canned corn is to can some of the sweetest corn you can find rather than adding sugar.

PROCESSING TIME: 55 MINUTES | **PRESSURE: 10 POUNDS WEIGHTED GAUGE, 11 POUNDS DIAL GAUGE**
YIELD: 3 PINTS

7 pounds fresh ears of corn, husks and silks removed

1½ teaspoons canning salt

1. Prepare 3 pint jars and the canner: Clean the jars and prepare the 2-piece lids according to the manufacturer's guidelines. Keep the jars in hot but not boiling water until you're ready to use them. Prepare the canner by filling it with 2 to 3 inches of water and bringing it to a simmer, or according to your manufacturer's directions.

2. Using a sharp knife, cut the corn kernels from the cobs. Cut about ¾ of the kernel to avoid cutting into the cob.

3. In a medium-size pot, bring at least 2 quarts of water to a boil.

4. In a large pot over medium heat, combine the corn kernels with 1 cup of boiling water for each 2 cups of corn. Bring the mixture to a simmer and cook for 5 minutes.

5. Using a slotted ladle or large slotted spoon, carefully ladle the corn evenly into the hot jars, leaving a bit more than 1 inch of headspace. Pour the hot cooking liquid over top, leaving 1 inch of headspace.

6. Add ½ teaspoon of salt to each pint jar.

7. Remove any air bubbles with a plastic or wooden utensil, adding more hot liquid as needed to maintain the proper 1-inch headspace.

8. Wipe the rims and seal the jars hand-tight with the 2-piece lids.

9. Carefully transfer the filled jars to the rack inside the pressure canner. Process the jars at the pressure listed above for 55 minutes.

10. Let the canner return to 0 pounds pressure. Wait 10 minutes more, then carefully open the canner lid according to the manufacturer's instructions.

11. With a jar lifter, remove the jars and place them on a clean dishtowel away from any drafts. Once the jars cool to room temperature, check the seals. If any jars have not sealed, refrigerate them and use the corn within 2 weeks. Label the remaining jars with the recipe name and date before storing.

CREAMED CORN

You'd be forgiven for thinking there was actual cream in this creamed corn, yet this is the perfect side dish for vegans or even the base for a creamy vegan soup. It's rich yet lighter than dairy-filled creamed corn, thanks to the goodness of the natural corn "milk." Corn milk? Yes, and getting what I call corn milk is easy: After you blanch the corn and remove the kernels, run the back of your knife down the cob. You can even catch all the milk in the same bowl as the kernels as you go. It might just become your new cooking secret!

PROCESSING TIME: 1 HOUR, 35 MINUTES | PRESSURE: 10 POUNDS WEIGHTED GAUGE, 11 POUNDS DIAL GAUGE YIELD: 3 PINTS

---

7 pounds fresh ears of corn, husks and silks removed

1½ teaspoons canning salt

1. Prepare 3 pint jars and the canner: Clean the jars and prepare the 2-piece lids according to the manufacturer's guidelines. Keep the jars in hot but not boiling water until you're ready to use them. Prepare the canner by filling it with 2 to 3 inches of water and bringing it to a simmer, or according to your manufacturer's directions.

2. In a large pot of boiling water (or more pots as needed) over high heat, blanch the corn on the cob for 4 minutes. Remove the corn and let the cobs cool enough to handle safely.

3. With a sharp knife, cut the corn kernels from the cobs. Cut about ¾ of the kernel to avoid cutting into the cob.

4. Run the back of your knife blade over the cob a second time to remove the corn "milk" and combine "milk" with kernels.

5. In a large pot over high heat, combine the corn kernels with 1 cup of water for every 2 cups corn–corn milk mixture. Bring the mixture to a boil.

6. In a separate pot over high heat, bring 2 quarts water to a boil in case you need more hot liquid to top up your jars.

7. Using a slotted ladle or large slotted spoon, carefully ladle the corn evenly into the hot jars, leaving a bit more than 1 inch of headspace. Pour the boiling water over the top, as needed, leaving 1 inch of headspace.

8. Add ½ teaspoon of salt to each pint jar.

9. Remove any air bubbles with a plastic or wooden utensil, adding more boiling water as needed to maintain the proper 1-inch headspace.

(continued)

10. Wipe the rims and seal the jars hand-tight with the 2-piece lids.

11. Carefully transfer the filled jars to the rack inside the pressure canner. Process the jars at the pressure listed above for 1 hour, 35 minutes.

12. Let the canner return to 0 pounds pressure. Wait 10 minutes more, then carefully open the canner lid according to the manufacturer's instructions.

13. With a jar lifter, remove the jars and place them on a clean dishtowel away from any drafts. Once the jars cool to room temperature, check the seals. If any jars have not sealed, refrigerate them and use the corn within 2 weeks. Label the remaining jars with the recipe name and date before storing.

CORN RELISH

Corn relish is a versatile condiment. It can be used like creamed corn—for a pop of summery flavor in the deep of winter. However, it's also a summer classic, found at backyard barbecues across the country. At my house, we eat it on our burgers, mixed into chicken salad, and some even take an extra spoonful or two for a bite on the side!

PROCESSING TIME: 20 MINUTES | **PRESSURE: 10 POUNDS WEIGHTED GAUGE, 11 POUNDS DIAL GAUGE**
YIELD: 6 PINTS

16 to 20 fresh ears of corn, husks and silks removed

2 cups chopped onion

1 cup chopped green bell pepper

¾ cup chopped red bell pepper

1½ cups sugar

1 quart white or apple cider vinegar, 5%

1 tablespoon dry mustard

1 tablespoon mustard seeds

2 tablespoons canning salt

1. Prepare 6 pint jars and the canner: Clean the jars and prepare the 2-piece lids according to the manufacturer's guidelines. Keep the jars in hot but not boiling water until you're ready to use them. Prepare the canner by filling it with 2 to 3 inches of water and bringing it to a simmer, or according to your manufacturer's directions.

2. With a sharp knife, cut the corn kernels from the ears until you have about 2 quarts of kernels.

3. In large pot over high heat, combine the corn, onion, green and red bell peppers, sugar, vinegar, dry mustard, mustard seeds, and canning salt. Bring to a boil, stirring occasionally.

4. Once the mixture reaches a boil, stir it again, cover the pot, and simmer for 20 minutes. Continue stirring occasionally to prevent scorching.

5. Carefully ladle the corn mixture into the hot jars, leaving 1 inch of headspace. You should have enough relish to fill your jars and there is no recommended top-up liquid for this recipe.

6. Remove any air bubbles with a plastic or wooden utensil, adding more relish as needed to maintain the proper 1-inch headspace.

7. Wipe the rims and seal the jars hand-tight with the 2-piece lids.

8. Carefully transfer the filled jars to the rack inside the pressure canner. Process the jars at the pressure listed above for 20 minutes.

9. Let the canner return to 0 pounds pressure. Wait 10 minutes more, then carefully open the canner lid according to the manufacturer's instructions.

10. With a jar lifter, remove the jars and place them on a clean dishtowel away from any drafts. Once the jars cool to room temperature, check the seals. If any jars have not sealed, refrigerate them and use the relish within 2 weeks. Label the remaining jars with the recipe name and date before storing.

PERFECTLY CANNED PEAS

Fresh peas are fun to pick and prepare. Stir-fry them, steam them, or snip the ends and eat 'em raw! However, almost nobody thinks of canning peas as the ideal way to treat these flavor-packed little morsels. I encourage you to get past the undeserved reputation of canned peas and try canning them at home. You'll soon find they're not mushy at all, and, in fact, pack nearly as much flavor as fresh peas. So, spread the word! Can those peas and share them with your friends.

**PROCESSING TIME: 40 MINUTES | PRESSURE: 10 POUNDS WEIGHTED GAUGE, 11 POUNDS DIAL GAUGE
YIELD: 3 PINTS**

7 pounds fresh peas in their pods, washed, and peas removed from the pods

1½ teaspoons canning salt

1. Prepare 3 pint jars and the canner: Clean the jars and prepare the 2-piece lids according to the manufacturer's guidelines. Keep the jars in hot but not boiling water until you're ready to use them. Prepare the canner by filling it with 2 to 3 inches of water and bringing it to a simmer, or according to your manufacturer's directions.

2. Place the peas in a large pot, cover them with water, and bring to a boil over high heat. Boil for 4 minutes, or until they are bright green but not completely cooked.

3. Drain the peas over a large pot or bowl to reserve the cooking liquid. Pack the cooked peas loosely into the prepared jars.

4. Pour the hot cooking liquid over the peas, leaving 1 inch of headspace.

5. Add ½ teaspoon of salt to each pint jar.

6. Remove any air bubbles with a plastic or wooden utensil, adding more hot cooking liquid as needed to maintain the proper 1-inch headspace.

7. Wipe the rims and seal the jars hand-tight with the 2-piece lids.

8. Carefully transfer the filled jars to the rack inside the pressure canner. Process the jars at the pressure listed above for 40 minutes.

9. Let the canner return to 0 pounds pressure. Wait 10 minutes more, then carefully open the canner lid according to the manufacturer's instructions.

10. With a jar lifter, remove the jars and place them on a clean dishtowel away from any drafts. Once the jars cool to room temperature, check the seals. If any jars have not sealed, refrigerate them and use the peas within 2 weeks. Label the remaining jars with the recipe name and date before storing.

SPICED PICKLED BEETS

If you're looking for a recipe that will make you famous with friends and family, look no further! While beets are healthy, they can sometimes be a tough sell to picky eaters, or younger eaters who complain they "taste like dirt." This recipe is sure to change minds as the beets receive a treatment of sugar, spice, and everything nice. For those who already love beets, it will be hard to eat just one. Serve them as part of an appetizer spread and watch them disappear.

PROCESSING TIME: 30 MINUTES | **PRESSURE: 10 POUNDS WEIGHTED GAUGE, 11 POUNDS DIAL GAUGE**
YIELD: 4 PINTS

4 pounds firm unblemished beets, washed, trimmed, leaving the root intact as well as about 2 inches of the stems

3 cups thinly sliced white onion

2 cups sugar

2½ cups distilled white vinegar

1½ cups water

1 teaspoon canning salt

2 tablespoons whole-spice pickling mix, or a mix of 1 tablespoon mustard seeds, 1 teaspoon whole allspice berries, 1 teaspoon whole cloves, and 3 cinnamon sticks

1. Prepare 4 pint jars and the canner: Clean the jars and prepare the 2-piece lids according to the manufacturer's guidelines. Keep the jars in hot but not boiling water until you're ready to use them. Prepare the canner by filling it with 2 to 3 inches of water and bringing it to a simmer, or according to your manufacturer's directions.

2. In a large pot, combine the beets with enough water to cover. Bring to a boil over high heat. Reduce the heat to low and simmer for about 20 minutes until fork-tender.

3. Drain the beets and run cold water over them to stop the cooking process. When cool enough to handle, use a sharp knife to remove the skins. The skins should easily come away from the flesh. Remove the stem and root at this point as well.

4. Slice the beets in ¼-inch-thick slices and place them in a large bowl. Set the beets aside.

5. Rinse the pot you cooked the beets in, place it over high heat, and combine the onion, sugar, vinegar, water, salt, and pickling mix in it. Bring the mixture to a boil. Reduce the heat to low and simmer for 5 minutes.

6. Add the beet slices to the hot mixture and simmer for 3 minutes more. Turn off the heat and remove the cinnamon sticks.

7. Carefully ladle the hot beet and onion mixture into the hot jars. Ladle the hot cooking liquid over the beets, leaving ½ inch of headspace.

8. Remove any air bubbles with a plastic or wooden utensil, adding more hot liquid as needed to maintain the proper ½-inch headspace.

(continued)

9. Wipe the rims and seal the jars hand-tight with the 2-piece lids.

10. Carefully transfer the filled jars to the rack inside the pressure canner. Process the jars at the pressure listed above for 30 minutes.

11. Let the canner return to 0 pounds pressure. Wait 10 minutes more, then carefully open the canner lid according to the manufacturer's instructions.

12. With a jar lifter, remove the jars and place them on a clean dishtowel away from any drafts. Once the jars cool to room temperature, check the seals. If any jars have not sealed, refrigerate them and use the beets within 2 weeks. Label the remaining jars with the recipe name and date before storing.

GREEN BEANS

In my garden I try to pick beans just as fast as they ripen. Fresh beans are the key to canning them and keeping a slight bite. If your beans have any bend, they will surely not be crisp after canning. While I previously cautioned about switching ingredients in and out of recipes, for this one you have my permission to use any color string-type bean you wish. They all taste great! Use these beans as a last-minute addition to your favorite stir-fry or soup. They will add a burst of fresh flavor to any dish.

**PROCESSING TIME: 20 MINUTES | PRESSURE: 10 POUNDS WEIGHTED GAUGE, 11 POUNDS DIAL GAUGE
YIELD: 4 PINTS**

1 pound green beans, ends trimmed and cut into 2-inch pieces

2 teaspoons canning salt

1. Prepare 4 pint jars and the canner: Clean the jars and prepare the 2-piece lids according to the manufacturer's guidelines. Keep the jars in hot but not boiling water until you're ready to use them. Prepare the canner by filling it with 2 to 3 inches of water and bringing it to a simmer, or according to your manufacturer's directions.

2. In a medium-size pot or kettle, bring 1 quart water to a boil.

3. While the water boils, pack the green beans into the hot jars as tightly as possible.

4. Pour the boiling water over the beans, leaving 1 inch of headspace.

5. Add ½ teaspoon of salt to each pint jar.

6. Remove any air bubbles with a plastic or wooden utensil, adding more boiling water as needed to maintain the proper 1-inch headspace.

7. Wipe the rims and seal the jars hand-tight with the 2-piece lids.

8. Carefully transfer the filled jars to the rack inside the pressure canner. Process the jars at the pressure listed above for 20 minutes.

9. Let the canner return to 0 pounds pressure. Wait 10 minutes more, then carefully open the canner lid according to the manufacturer's instructions.

10. With a jar lifter, remove the jars and place them on a clean dishtowel away from any drafts. Once the jars cool to room temperature, check the seals. If any jars have not sealed, refrigerate them and use the vegetables within 2 weeks. Label the remaining jars with the recipe name and date before storing.

SPICY DILLY BEANS

Pickled green beans, also known as dilly beans in some circles, are a must-have for your pantry. They make a tangy component of bean salads, but they also work great as a condiment and as a unique topping for appetizers. Some even swear by them as a garnish for a Bloody Mary, used in place of the more traditional celery stalk. Mixing green and yellow beans adds a pop of color to the jars, but no matter the visual interest, these beans are tasty. You may not be able to make enough of them to last all year!

PROCESSING TIME: 20 MINUTES | PRESSURE: 10 POUNDS WEIGHTED GAUGE, 11 POUNDS DIAL GAUGE
YIELD: 4 PINTS

2½ cups distilled white vinegar

2½ cups water

¼ cup canning salt

2½ pounds green beans, ends trimmed; measured and cut so they leave ¼-inch headspace in the jars

4 garlic cloves, peeled

4 stems fresh dill, cut in half if tall

4 dried red chile peppers

1 teaspoon cayenne pepper

1 teaspoon dill seed

1. Prepare 4 pint jars and the canner: Clean the jars and prepare the 2-piece lids according to the manufacturer's guidelines. Keep the jars in hot but not boiling water until you're ready to use them. Prepare the canner by filling it with 2 to 3 inches of water and bringing it to a simmer, or according to your manufacturer's directions.

2. In a large pot over high heat, combine the vinegar, water, and salt. Bring the mixture to a boil and cook for 1 minute. Stir well while the mixture boils to make sure the salt dissolves. Reduce the heat to maintain a simmer and keep the liquid very hot while you continue to work.

3. Pack the beans upright in the jars, leaving ¼ inch of headspace. Cut the beans again, as needed, to leave the ¼ inch of headspace.

4. In each jar, place 1 clove garlic, 1 dill sprig, 1 dried red chile pepper, ¼ teaspoon of cayenne, and ¼ teaspoon of dill seed.

5. Carefully ladle the hot liquid over the beans, leaving ¼ inch of headspace.

6. Remove any air bubbles with a plastic or wooden utensil, adding more hot liquid as needed to maintain the proper ¼-inch headspace.

7. Wipe the rims and seal the jars hand-tight with the 2-piece lids.

8. Carefully transfer the filled jars to the rack inside the pressure canner. Process the jars at the pressure listed above for 20 minutes.

9. Let the canner return to 0 pounds pressure. Wait 10 minutes more, then carefully open the canner lid according to the manufacturer's instructions.

10. With a jar lifter, remove the jars and place them on a clean dishtowel away from any drafts. Once the jars cool to room temperature, check the seals. If any jars have not sealed, refrigerate them and use the beans within 2 weeks. Label the remaining jars with the recipe name and date before storing.

PICNIC-FRIENDLY BAKED BEANS

The problem with store-bought baked beans isn't the taste or the lack of variety. These days you can find maple baked beans, baked beans with thick-cut bacon, vegetarian baked beans—the list goes on! However, so many recipes contain questionable preservatives or flavor enhancers. Even the best recipes contain a large amount of sugar or other sweetener. You'll find this recipe makes beans with just the right amount of sweetness. The sauce is rich and the beans themselves still have some texture (something rarely said for store-bought baked beans). Serve alongside sandwiches and lemonade at your next picnic, or plan an indoor "picnic" night in the middle of winter. Hot dogs, hamburgers, corn, coleslaw, and these baked beans are always a treat.

Note that this recipe requires soaking the beans for 12 hours before cooking and canning. You'll also need to bake the bean recipe for about 3 hours, so it's a good idea to soak the beans the night before you want to cook and can them.

PROCESSING TIME: 1 HOUR, 20 MINUTES | PRESSURE: 10 POUNDS WEIGHTED GAUGE, 11 POUNDS DIAL GAUGE YIELD: 6 PINTS

---

2 pounds dried navy beans

6 quarts water

½ pound bacon, cut into small pieces

3 large onions, sliced

⅔ cup packed brown sugar

4 teaspoons salt

2 teaspoons dry mustard

⅓ cup molasses

1. The night before you want to can, place the beans into a large pot. Add 3 quarts of water to cover the beans. Soak the beans, covered, for 12 hours.

2. Drain the beans and return them to the pot. Add the remaining 3 quarts of water and bring the mixture to a boil over high heat. Reduce the heat to low and simmer the beans until soft and the skins begin to split, about 1½ to 2 hours. Drain the beans and reserve the cooking liquid.

3. Preheat the oven to 350°F.

4. Transfer the drained beans to a large baking dish and add the bacon and onions.

5. In large bowl, stir together the brown sugar, salt, dry mustard, and molasses. Add 4 cups of the reserved cooking liquid (add more water if needed to make 4 cups). Stir this sauce until it is well combined. Pour the sauce over the beans—but do not stir. Cover the dish with aluminum foil and bake for 3½ hours.

6. Meanwhile, prepare 6 pint jars and the canner: Clean the jars and prepare the 2-piece lids according to the manufacturer's guidelines. Keep the jars in hot but not boiling water until you're ready to use them. Prepare the canner by filling it with 2 to 3 inches of water and bringing it to a simmer, or according to your manufacturer's directions.

(continued)

7. After 3½ hours, carefully ladle the bean into the hot jars, leaving 1 inch of headspace.

8. Remove any air bubbles with a plastic or wooden utensil, adding more beans as needed to maintain the proper 1-inch headspace.

9. Wipe the rims and seal the jars hand-tight with the 2-piece lids.

10. Carefully transfer the filled jars to the rack inside the pressure canner. Process the jars at the pressure listed above for 1 hour, 20 minutes.

11. Let the canner return to 0 pounds pressure. Wait 10 minutes more, then carefully open the canner lid according to the manufacturer's instructions.

12. With a jar lifter, remove the jars and place them on a clean dishtowel away from any drafts. Once the jars cool to room temperature, check the seals. If any jars have not sealed, refrigerate them and use the beans within 2 weeks. Label the remaining jars with the recipe name and date before storing.

HEIRLOOM BEANS

Dried beans are practically magical. They are inexpensive and filling, and can give a hearty boost to many recipes. You can even combine them with rice for a complete protein. If there's one downside they have, it's the time. Chances are, you reach much more for canned beans than dried on a daily basis—so why not can your own? While you can certainly use any dried beans you have on hand for this recipe, I recommend seeking out an heirloom bean to elevate this pantry staple. There are so many bean varieties you can order these days, and most are not available as canned beans in the grocery store! It is not necessary to add the salt pork or bacon, but it's a great way to infuse additional flavor into your beans and separate them from their store-bought counterparts. If you omit the salt pork or bacon, add a little salt, or not, depending on how you like to use your beans in recipes.

Just like the Picnic-Friendly Baked Beans (page 75), these beans require an overnight (12-hour) soak before you're ready to cook and can.

PROCESSING TIME: 1 HOUR, 35 MINUTES | PRESSURE: 10 POUNDS WEIGHTED GAUGE, 11 POUNDS DIAL GAUGE YIELD: 3 PINTS

8 ounces dried beans of choice

½ cup cubed salt pork, or ¼ pound good bacon, cut into bite-size pieces (optional; see headnote)

1. The night before you want to can, place the beans in large pot and cover them with warm water. Soak the beans, covered, for 12 hours.

2. Drain the beans, return them to the pot, and cover them with fresh water. Cook over medium-high heat until they begin to boil. Stir and continue cooking the beans according to the package directions, but stop just short of cooking them all the way through.

3. Meanwhile, prepare 3 pint jars and the canner: Clean the jars and prepare the 2-piece lids according to the manufacturer's guidelines. Keep the jars in hot but not boiling water until you're ready to use them. Prepare the canner by filling it with 2 to 3 inches of water and bringing it to a simmer, or according to your manufacturer's directions.

4. Meanwhile, bring 1 quart of water to a boil in case you need more hot liquid to top up your jars. (Some beans absorb more water than others while cooking.)

5. Divide the salt pork, or bacon, evenly among the pint jars (if using).

6. Carefully ladle the hot beans into the hot jars. Pour the hot cooking liquid over the top, leaving 1 inch of headspace. If the cooking liquid does not go far enough, add the hot water to top up to the proper 1-inch headspace.

(continued)

7. Remove any air bubbles with a plastic or wooden utensil, adding more hot liquid as needed to maintain the proper 1-inch headspace.

8. Wipe the rims and seal the jars hand-tight with the 2-piece lids.

9. Carefully transfer the filled jars to the rack inside the pressure canner. Process the jars at the pressure listed above for 1 hour, 35 minutes.

10. Let the canner return to 0 pounds pressure. Wait 10 minutes more, then carefully open the canner lid according to the manufacturer's instructions.

11. With a jar lifter, remove the jars and place them on a clean dishtowel away from any drafts. Once the jars cool to room temperature, check the seals. If any jars have not sealed, refrigerate them and use the beans within 2 weeks. Label the remaining jars with the recipe name and date before storing.

LENTILS

Lentils are a popular base for healthy soup recipes. There are also many varieties of lentil salad, from Middle Eastern preparations to American classics. Unlike most beans, lentils do not need a long soak before cooking and that means there's no need to soak them before canning either. While lentils are one of the quicker legumes to cook from scratch, there's nothing as quick as cracking open a jar of your homemade canned lentils!

PROCESSING TIME: 1 HOUR, 15 MINUTES | PRESSURE: 10 POUNDS WEIGHTED GAUGE, 11 POUNDS DIAL GAUGE YIELD: 3 PINTS

2 cups dried lentils

4 cups Vegetable Broth (page 185) or store-bought broth

1 large onion, minced

1. Prepare 3 pint jars and the canner: Clean the jars and prepare the 2-piece lids according to the manufacturer's guidelines. Keep the jars in hot but not boiling water until you're ready to use them. Prepare the canner by filling it with 2 to 3 inches of water and bringing it to a simmer, or according to your manufacturer's directions.

2. Inspect the lentils carefully and remove any foreign objects, such as small stones. Place the lentils in a large pot and add the broth and onion. Bring the pot to a boil over high heat, reduce the heat, and simmer for about 5 minutes until the lentils are partially cooked.

3. Carefully ladle the lentils into the hot jars, filling each jar halfway. Ladle the hot cooking liquid over the lentils, leaving 1 inch of headspace in the jars.

4. Remove any air bubbles with a plastic or wooden utensil, adding more hot cooking liquid as needed to maintain the proper headspace.

5. Wipe the rims and seal the jars hand-tight with the 2-piece lids.

6. Carefully transfer the filled jars to the rack inside the pressure canner. Process the jars at the pressure listed above for 1 hour, 15 minutes.

7. Let the canner return to 0 pounds pressure. Wait 10 minutes more, then carefully open the canner lid according to the manufacturer's instructions.

8. With a jar lifter, remove the jars and place them on a clean dishtowel away from any drafts. Once the jars cool to room temperature, check the seals. If any jars have not sealed, refrigerate them and use the lentils within 2 weeks. Label the remaining jars with the recipe name and date before storing.

KIDNEY BEAN SOUP

Canned bean soups are a lot like canned beans—they can get the job done, but it's hard to get excited about them. Worse even, canned soups often pack lots of sodium—perhaps making up for their shortcomings in texture or flavor! This soup is a clear upgrade and, even better, kid approved. One of my family's favorite meals is a combination of this soup with fresh-from-the-oven biscuits. I've also done some testing and this recipe holds up just fine if you want to omit the ham and use vegetable broth instead of a meat-based broth. As far as the salt goes, I recommend canning this recipe as is and allowing your family (or guests) to season with salt and pepper when serving. The salt in the broth may well be enough for some.

PROCESSING TIME: 1 HOUR | **PRESSURE: 10 POUNDS WEIGHTED GAUGE, 11 POUNDS DIAL GAUGE**
YIELD: 4 PINTS

2 quarts Chicken or Turkey Broth (page 177) or store-bought broth

1 cup diced peeled potatoes

1 cup fresh corn kernels

½ cup sliced celery

½ large yellow onion, diced

1 garlic clove, thinly sliced

1 cup cubed cooked ham

1 cup canned and drained kidney beans

1. In a large stockpot over medium-high heat, combine the broth, potatoes, corn, celery, onion, and garlic. Cover the pot and heat until the mixture comes to a simmer.

2. Add the ham and kidney beans. Bring the mixture to a boil. Cook for 10 minutes.

3. Meanwhile, prepare 4 pint jars and the canner: Clean the jars and prepare the 2-piece lids according to the manufacturer's guidelines. Keep the jars in hot but not boiling water until you're ready to use them. Prepare the canner by filling it with 2 to 3 inches of water and bringing it to a simmer, or according to your manufacturer's directions.

4. Carefully ladle the hot soup into the hot jars, leaving 1 inch of headspace.

5. Wipe the rims and seal the jars hand-tight with the 2-piece lids.

6. Carefully transfer the filled jars to the rack inside the pressure canner. Process the jars at the pressure listed above for 1 hour.

7. Let the canner return to 0 pounds pressure. Wait 10 minutes more, then carefully open the canner lid according to the manufacturer's instructions.

8. With a jar lifter, remove the jars and place them on a clean dishtowel away from any drafts. Once the jars cool to room temperature, check the seals. If any jars have not sealed, refrigerate them and use the soup within 2 weeks. Label the remaining jars with the recipe name and date before storing.

MIXED VEGETABLE MEDLEY

When I was a little girl, whenever my family had mixed vegetables I picked out every piece of mushy carrot. Now that I make them myself, I make sure every vegetable is ripe so the whole mixture is delicious. I'm happy to say my kids don't leave any vegetable behind! One quick note: make sure to wash and dice your vegetables to a uniform size before combining them to cook, or they may not cook at the same speed. Beyond making for an easy out-of-the-jar side dish, mixed vegetables are great to have on hand for soups or as a topping for healthy grain bowls.

PROCESSING TIME: 55 MINUTES | PRESSURE: 10 POUNDS WEIGHTED GAUGE, 11 POUNDS DIAL GAUGE
YIELD: 4 PINTS

1 cup chopped tomatoes

7 cups total of a combination of the following, all cut to uniform sizes (see headnote):

Diced carrots (1-inch dice)

Sweet corn

Green beans, cut into 1-inch pieces

Diced zucchini (1-inch dice)

2 teaspoons canning salt

1. Prepare 4 pint jars and the canner: Clean the jars and prepare the 2-piece lids according to the manufacturer's guidelines. Keep the jars in hot but not boiling water until you're ready to use them. Prepare the canner by filling it with 2 to 3 inches of water and bringing it to a simmer, or according to your manufacturer's directions.

2. In a large pot, combine the tomatoes with the 7 cups of vegetables you selected and add enough water to cover. Bring the mixture to a boil over high heat and boil for 5 minutes. Stir frequently to prevent any burning or sticking on the bottom of the pot.

3. Carefully ladle the vegetables evenly into the hot jars. Top with the hot cooking liquid, leaving 1 inch of headspace.

4. Add ½ teaspoon of salt to each jar.

5. Remove any air bubbles with a plastic or wooden utensil, adding more hot liquid as needed to maintain the proper 1-inch headspace.

6. Wipe the rims and seal the jars hand-tight with the 2-piece lids.

7. Carefully transfer the filled jars to the rack inside the pressure canner Process the jars at the pressure listed above for 55 minutes.

8. Let the canner return to 0 pounds pressure. Wait 10 minutes more, then carefully open the canner lid according to the manufacturer's instructions.

9. With a jar lifter, remove the jars and place them on a clean dishtowel away from any drafts. Once the jars cool to room temperature, check the seals. If any jars have not sealed, refrigerate them and use the vegetables within 2 weeks. Label the remaining jars with the recipe name and date before storing.

CANNED POTATOES

I know fall has arrived when the potato man comes down from Aroostook County to sell his potatoes by the 50-pound bag—50 pounds! I buy two bags, one for my shelves and one for dry storage. Canning potatoes is one concept that can take some getting used to, as they're not a popular product in most grocery stores. However, I think once you start canning them you'll be converted. You can use the potatoes in nearly all the recipes you'd normally cook—except baked potatoes, of course! Having them precooked just means less time cooking dinner. Add them to soups and chowders or throw them on a sheet tray for roasting along with some quick-cooking vegetables. Since you just have to crisp the potatoes and not cook them from scratch, dinner is ready in no time.

PROCESSING TIME: 35 MINUTES | PRESSURE: 10 POUNDS WEIGHTED GAUGE, 11 POUNDS DIAL GAUGE
YIELD: 6 PINTS

3 pounds fresh potatoes, washed, peeled, and cut into ½-inch cubes

3 teaspoons canning salt

1. Prepare 6 pint jars and the canner: Clean the jars and prepare the 2-piece lids according to the manufacturer's guidelines. Keep the jars in hot but not boiling water until you're ready to use them. Prepare the canner by filling it with 2 to 3 inches of water and bringing it to a simmer, or according to your manufacturer's directions.

2. In a large pot over high heat, bring 1 gallon of water to a boil.

3. Place the potatoes into the boiling water. Return the water to a boil and cook for 2 minutes.

4. Using a large slotted spoon, pack the potatoes into the hot jars. Reserve the cooking liquid.

5. Add ½ teaspoon of salt to each jar.

6. Ladle the hot cooking liquid over the potatoes, leaving 1 inch of headspace.

7. Remove air bubbles with a plastic or wooden utensil, adding more hot liquid as needed to maintain the proper 1-inch headspace.

8. Wipe the rims and seal the jars hand-tight with the 2-piece lids.

9. Carefully transfer the filled jars to the rack inside the pressure canner. Process the jars at the pressure listed above for 35 minutes.

10. Let the canner return to 0 pounds pressure. Wait 10 minutes more, then carefully open the canner lid according to the manufacturer's instructions.

11. With a jar lifter, remove the jars and place them on a clean dishtowel away from any drafts. Once the jars cool to room temperature, check the seals. If any jars have not sealed, refrigerate them and use the potatoes within 2 weeks. Label the remaining jars with the recipe name and date before storing.

TASTE OF SUMMER CARROT STICKS

You might think canned carrot sticks would take away the fun of snapping into a fresh carrot, as you cook out some of the crunch. However, carrots take on a new flavor profile when canned. Cooked just enough to enhance the natural sweetness, canned carrot sticks are a healthy finger food whenever you need to mix up snack time.

PROCESSING TIME: 25 MINUTES | PRESSURE: 10 POUNDS WEIGHTED GAUGE, 11 POUNDS DIAL GAUGE
YIELD: 3 PINTS

6 pounds whole carrots, washed and peeled

1½ teaspoons canning salt

1. Prepare 3 pint jars and the canner: Clean the jars and prepare the 2-piece lids according to the manufacturer's guidelines. Keep the jars in hot but not boiling water until you're ready to use them. Prepare the canner by filling it with 2 to 3 inches of water and bringing it to a simmer, or according to your manufacturer's directions.

2. Cut the carrots into sticks very close to the same size, long enough to fit into the jars leaving 1 inch of headspace.

3. Place the carrot sticks in a large saucepan and cover them with water. Bring to a boil over high heat, reduce the heat to a simmer, and cook for 5 minutes.

4. In another saucepan, bring a few cups of water to a boil as a reserve, if needed, to fill the jars to the proper headspace.

5. Tightly pack the carrots into the hot jars, leaving 1 inch of headspace.

6. Add ½ teaspoon of salt to each pint jar.

7. Ladle the hot cooking liquid over the carrots, leaving 1 inch of headspace.

8. Remove any air bubbles with a plastic or wooden utensil, adding the reserved hot water as needed to maintain the proper 1-inch headspace.

9. Wipe the rims and seal the jars hand-tight with the 2-piece lids.

10. Carefully transfer the filled jars to the rack inside the pressure canner. Process the jars at the pressure listed above for 25 minutes.

11. Let the canner return to 0 pounds pressure. Wait 10 minutes more, then carefully open the canner lid according to the manufacturer's instructions.

12. With a jar lifter, remove the jars and place them on a clean dishtowel away from any drafts. Once the jars cool to room temperature, check the seals. If any jars have not sealed, refrigerate them and use the carrots within 2 weeks. Label the remaining jars with the recipe name and date before storing.

CHAPTER FOUR

GOING FURTHER WITH VEGETABLES

I'M A BELIEVER IN KEEPING IT SIMPLE, especially when you're just starting out. Instead of trying to find fifty recipes with fifty different vegetables, it's more interesting and rewarding to focus on a dozen vegetables that grow well in your area and different ways to prepare them. As you return to the same season year after year, you'll naturally build on what you learned the year before.

Yet simple doesn't mean boring! From the first asparagus of the season to the last fall pumpkin, pressure canning unexpected vegetables is a wonderful way to preserve your garden's bounty—beyond peas, corn, and carrots. In fact, I've found that some of these more unusual vegetables—fiddlehead ferns, for example—make great food gifts with a real wow factor.

In this chapter, you'll also find new ideas for more common vegetables—Sweet and Spicy Ginger Carrot Coins (page 91) with an unexpected hit of ginger, onions are re-imagined as The Perfect Cocktail Onions (page 95), and zucchini takes a trip to Hawaii where it's married with the flavor of pineapple (page 106). (It may sound crazy, but it really works!) These recipes will take your excitement for canning to a new level.

SWEET AND SPICY GINGER CARROT COINS

If you want a carrot recipe with some kick, you've come to the right place. In this recipe, the sweetness from brown sugar and orange juice marries with spicy ginger, making these carrots your new favorite finger food. I've also made this recipe with baby carrots instead of carrot coins with great results. They are fantastic for a party!

PROCESSING TIME: 30 MINUTES | **PRESSURE: 10 POUNDS WEIGHTED GAUGE, 11 POUNDS DIAL GAUGE**
YIELD: 4 PINTS

2½ pounds carrots, washed and peeled

2 cups packed brown sugar

1 cup freshly squeezed orange juice (from 2 to 4 oranges)

2 cups water

2 pieces crystallized ginger (about 1 inch each), minced

1. Prepare 4 pint jars and the canner: Clean the jars and prepare the 2-piece lids according to the manufacturer's guidelines. Keep the jars in hot but not boiling water until you're ready to use them. Prepare the canner by filling it with 2 to 3 inches of water and bringing it to a simmer, or according to your manufacturer's directions.

2. Cut the carrots into ⅓-inch-thick coins or 1-inch chunks, unless you're using baby carrots, which you can process whole.

3. In a large saucepan over medium heat, combine the brown sugar, orange juice, water, and crystallized ginger. Cook until the sugar dissolves. Keep the syrup hot, stirring occasionally, as you continue to work. Reduce the heat if the mixture comes close to a simmer.

4. Pack the carrots tightly into the hot jars, leaving 1 inch of headspace.

5. Carefully ladle the hot syrup over the carrots. Leave 1 inch of headspace.

6. Remove any air bubbles with a plastic or wooden utensil, adding more hot syrup as needed to maintain the proper 1-inch headspace.

7. Wipe the rims and seal the jars hand-tight with the 2-piece lids.

8. Carefully transfer the filled jars to the rack inside the pressure canner. Process the jars at the pressure listed above for 30 minutes.

9. Let the canner return to 0 pounds pressure. Wait 10 minutes more, then carefully open the canner lid according to the manufacturer's instructions.

10. With a jar lifter, remove the jars and place them on a clean dishtowel away from any drafts. Once the jars cool to room temperature, check the seals. If any jars have not sealed, refrigerate them and use the carrots within 2 weeks. Label the remaining jars with the recipe name and date before storing.

FIRST-OF-THE-SEASON ASPARAGUS

Asparagus is one of the first signs of spring on our farm. Once you find these pencil-thin spears in the garden or at the farmers' market, it's officially time to get out the canner and jars. Canning asparagus is easy to do, though it takes practice to pack the jars. You need to fit enough to fill the jars, but you don't want to overpack them—and of course the spears can be too tall for the jars! If you're planning to gift some of the jars, make them especially beautiful by placing the best-looking spears around the outside of the jar where they will show. Then the not-as-pretty, but still delicious, spears will be in the center. If you don't care about the appearance of the asparagus in the jars, cut it up and fill the jars with bite-size pieces instead. It tastes every bit as good and is much easier to pack.

**PROCESSING TIME: 30 MINUTES | PRESSURE: 10 POUNDS WEIGHTED GAUGE, 11 POUNDS DIAL GAUGE
YIELD: 4 PINTS**

8 pounds fresh asparagus, washed and trimmed to fit the height of the jars (they shrink in the canning process)

2 teaspoons canning salt

1. Prepare 4 pint jars and the canner: Clean the jars and prepare the 2-piece lids according to the manufacturer's guidelines. Keep the jars in hot but not boiling water until you're ready to use them. Prepare the canner by filling it with 2 to 3 inches of water and bringing it to a simmer, or according to your manufacturer's directions.

2. In a large pot over high heat, bring 2 quarts water to a boil.

3. Pack the raw asparagus spears into the hot jars as tightly as possible.

4. Add ½ teaspoon of salt to each pint jar.

5. Using a funnel or ladle, carefully add boiling water to each jar leaving 1 inch of headspace.

6. Remove air bubbles with a plastic or wooden utensil, adding more hot water as needed to maintain the proper 1-inch headspace.

7. Wipe the rims and seal the jars hand-tight with the 2-piece lids.

8. Carefully transfer the filled jars to the rack inside the pressure canner. Process the jars at the pressure listed above for 30 minutes.

9. Let the canner return to 0 pounds pressure. Wait 10 minutes more, then carefully open the canner lid according to the manufacturer's instructions.

10. With a jar lifter, remove the jars and place them on a clean dishtowel away from any drafts. Once the jars cool to room temperature, check the seals. If any jars have not sealed, refrigerate them and use the asparagus within 2 weeks. Label the remaining jars with the recipe name and date before storing.

THE PERFECT COCKTAIL ONIONS

If you love cocktail hour, it's time to bring some of your favorite canning recipes to the bar. Many recipes in this book can do double duty as a happy hour snack, but a few recipes work as a cocktail garnish as well. Most often called pearl onions, these beautiful minis are especially delicious when pickled to perfection. My subtle variation on this classic recipe is to add a garlic clove to each jar. I think that extra complexity creates a depth of flavor, but feel free to leave out the garlic if desired.

PROCESSING TIME: 11 MINUTES | PRESSURE: 10 POUNDS WEIGHTED GAUGE, 11 POUNDS DIAL GAUGE
YIELD: 4 PINTS

5½ cups distilled white vinegar

1 cup water

2 cups sugar

2 teaspoons canning salt

8 cups white pearl onions, peeled and washed

4 garlic cloves, peeled (optional)

8 teaspoons mustard seeds

4 teaspoons celery seed

1. Prepare 4 pint jars and the canner: Clean the jars and prepare the 2-piece lids according to the manufacturer's guidelines. Keep the jars in hot but not boiling water until you're ready to use them. Prepare the canner by filling it with 2 to 3 inches of water and bringing it to a simmer, or according to your manufacturer's directions.

2. In a large pot over medium-high heat, combine the vinegar, water, sugar, and salt. Bring to a boil, and boil for 5 minutes.

3. Add the onions, reduce the heat to a simmer, and cook for 5 minutes more.

4. Place the following into each hot jar: 1 garlic clove (if using), 2 teaspoons mustard seeds, and 1 teaspoon celery seed.

5. Using a slotted spoon, remove the onions from their cooking liquid (reserve the liquid for filling the jars) and firmly pack them into the prepared jars.

6. Carefully pour the hot cooking liquid over the onions, leaving 1 inch of headspace.

7. Release any air bubbles with a plastic or wooden utensil, adding more hot liquid as necessary to maintain the proper 1-inch headspace.

8. Wipe the rims and seal the jars hand-tight with the 2-piece lids.

9. Carefully transfer the filled jars to the rack inside the pressure canner. Process the jars at the pressure listed above for 11 minutes.

10. Let the canner return to 0 pounds pressure. Wait 10 minutes more, then carefully open the canner lid according to the manufacturer's instructions.

11. With a jar lifter, remove the jars and place them on a clean dishtowel away from any drafts. Once the jars cool to room temperature, check the seals. If any jars have not sealed, refrigerate them and use the onions within 2 weeks. Label the remaining jars with the recipe name and date before storing.

YEAR-ROUND PUMPKIN BITES

In my opinion pumpkin isn't as popular as it should be. Sure, there's the annual pumpkin spice madness come fall, where you can find "pumpkin" in everything from lattes to candles. However, the enthusiasm seems to be more about the spice than the pumpkin. By preserving cubes of this vitamin A–rich vegetable without typical pie spices, you taste the natural flavor of the pumpkin all the better. Though this recipe uses light sugar syrup to bring out the sweetness of the pumpkin, the jars can be used for more than just desserts. Try pumpkin anywhere you'd use sweet squash, such as in soups, grain bowls, or as a side dish garnished with fresh herbs.

PROCESSING TIME: 30 MINUTES | PRESSURE: 10 POUNDS WEIGHTED GAUGE, 11 POUNDS DIAL GAUGE
YIELD: 6 PINTS

1 recipe light sugar syrup (see page 114)

10 pounds pie (sugar) pumpkins, halved, peeled, seeds and pulp removed, cut into 1-inch cubes

1. Prepare 6 pint jars and the canner: Clean the jars and prepare the 2-piece lids according to the manufacturer's guidelines. Keep the jars in hot but not boiling water until you're ready to use them. Prepare the canner by filling it with 2 to 3 inches of water and bringing it to a simmer, or according to your manufacturer's directions.

2. In a medium-size saucepan over high heat, bring the light sugar syrup to a boil.

3. Pack the raw pumpkin into the hot jars.

4. Carefully pour or ladle the hot syrup over the pumpkin, leaving 1 inch of headspace.

5. Remove air bubbles with a plastic or wooden utensil, adding more hot syrup as needed to maintain the proper 1-inch headspace.

6. Wipe the rims and seal the jars hand-tight with the 2-piece lids.

7. Carefully transfer the filled jars to the rack inside the pressure canner. Process the jars at the pressure listed above for 30 minutes.

8. Let the canner return to 0 pounds pressure. Wait 10 minutes more, then carefully open the canner lid according to the manufacturer's instructions.

9. With a jar lifter, remove the jars and place them on a clean dishtowel away from any drafts. Once the jars cool to room temperature, check the seals. If any jars have not sealed, refrigerate them and use the pumpkin within 2 weeks. Label the remaining jars with the recipe name and date before storing.

SPICY HOT PEPPER MIX

It seems as though every family has at least one eater who wants—no, needs—to turn the heat up. Yet what constitutes spicy varies not only from person to person but also family to family. My family's "hot" might seem mild to you! The nice thing about this recipe is that it can be dialed up or down when it comes to heat. Make a batch of habaneros for the capsaicin hound in your house or seed jalapeños and serranos from the garden for a milder mix. If your pepper mix turns out too hot, there's a way to soften the edge after processing. Chop some Taste of Summer Carrot Sticks (page 87) and mix them in a bowl with your peppers for a homemade riff on a classic taqueria condiment.

You may want to start this recipe the night before, as you need 12 hours to soak the peppers before canning.

PROCESSING TIME: 15 MINUTES | **PRESSURE: 10 POUNDS WEIGHTED GAUGE, 11 POUNDS DIAL GAUGE**
YIELD: 3 PINTS

3 quarts assorted hot peppers

¾ cup canning salt

5 cups distilled white vinegar

1 cup water

¼ cup sugar

2 or 3 garlic cloves, sliced

1. Wearing rubber gloves, wash the peppers and cut 2 slits lengthwise into each pepper.

2. In a very large bowl or large pot, combine the salt with 1 gallon water. Stir to dissolve the salt completely. Add the peppers and let sit for 12 hours.

3. Prepare 3 pint jars and the canner: Clean the jars and prepare the 2-piece lids according to the manufacturer's guidelines. Keep the jars in hot but not boiling water until you're ready to use them. Prepare the canner by filling it with 2 to 3 inches of water and bringing it to a simmer, or according to your manufacturer's directions.

4. Drain and rinse the peppers, and pack them into the hot jars.

5. In a medium-size saucepan over medium heat, combine the vinegar, water, sugar, and garlic. Bring to a simmer and cook for 15 minutes. Remove and discard the garlic. Carefully pour the hot solution over the peppers, leaving ½ inch of headspace.

6. Remove air bubbles with a plastic or wooden utensil, adding more hot liquid as needed to maintain the proper ½-inch headspace.

7. Wipe the rims and seal the jars hand-tight with the 2-piece lids.

(continued)

8. Carefully transfer the filled jars to the rack inside the pressure canner. Process the jars at the pressure listed above for 15 minutes.

9. Let the canner return to 0 pounds pressure. Wait 10 minutes more, then carefully open the canner lid according to the manufacturer's instructions.

10. With a jar lifter, remove the jars and place them on a clean dishtowel away from any drafts. Once the jars cool to room temperature, check the seals. If any jars have not sealed, refrigerate them and use the peppers within 2 weeks. Label the remaining jars with the recipe name and date before storing.

PICKLED CAULIFLOWER

Cauliflower is one versatile vegetable. It can be steamed and puréed for those who prefer it creamy. It can be riced or finely chopped, cooked for only a moment, and used in place of rice. It can be roasted, grilled, or tempura-battered and fried. Yet, unless you can, you probably haven't experienced the joy of tart, pickled cauliflower. While this recipe is so delicious it should be eaten straight from the jar, or as part of a cheese board, pickled cauliflower can also be a secret weapon. Imagine adding the crunch and tang of a homemade pickle, but without the cucumber flavor. I've found finely chopped pickled cauliflower is a welcome addition to potato salad, pasta salad, and even chicken salad.

PROCESSING TIME: 20 MINUTES | PRESSURE: 10 POUNDS WEIGHTED GAUGE, 11 POUNDS DIAL GAUGE
YIELD: 4 PINTS

4 cups water

4 cups distilled white vinegar

½ cup canning salt

4 pounds cauliflower, washed and cut into bite-size pieces, core discarded

1 yellow onion, sliced into ¼-inch-thick slices, breaking up any rings

1 teaspoon red pepper flakes

4 sprigs dill

4 garlic cloves, peeled

1. Prepare 4 pint jars and the canner: Clean the jars and prepare the 2-piece lids according to the manufacturer's guidelines. Keep the jars in hot but not boiling water until you're ready to use them. Prepare the canner by filling it with 2 to 3 inches of water and bringing it to a simmer, or according to your manufacturer's directions.

2. In a large pot over high heat, combine the water, vinegar, and salt. Bring the liquid to a boil and boil for 1 minute. Stir well to dissolve the salt completely. Reduce the heat to a simmer and keep the liquid very hot.

3. Fill each jar with cauliflower pieces and evenly divide the onion among the jars.

4. To each jar, add ¼ teaspoon red pepper flakes, 1 sprig dill, and 1 garlic clove.

5. Carefully ladle the hot liquid over the vegetables, leaving ¼ inch of headspace.

6. Remove air bubbles with a plastic or wooden utensil, adding more hot liquid as needed to maintain the proper ¼-inch headspace.

7. Wipe the rims and seal the jars hand-tight with the 2-piece lids.

8. Carefully transfer the filled jars to the rack inside the pressure canner. Process the jars at the pressure listed above for 20 minutes.

9. Let the canner return to 0 pounds pressure. Wait 10 minutes more, then carefully open the canner lid according to the manufacturer's instructions.

(continued)

10. With a jar lifter, remove the jars and place them on a clean dishtowel away from any drafts. Once the jars cool to room temperature, check the seals. If any jars have not sealed, refrigerate them and use the cauliflower within 2 weeks. Label the remaining jars with the recipe name and date before storing.

TOMATILLOS

When we lived in Nebraska, I grew both green and purple tomatillos for the farmers' market. Some customers had a little trepidation—after all, tomatillos are much less common than tomatoes in that part of the country. However, once I shared a few recipes for salsa verde and Mexican-inspired soups, people were hooked. Soon I couldn't grow enough to keep up with demand! While it's true you can make and pressure can salsa (see page 161), by canning the tomatillos as simply as possible, you'll have all options available when you crack open the jar.

PROCESSING TIME: 10 MINUTES | PRESSURE: 10 POUNDS WEIGHTED GAUGE, 11 POUNDS DIAL GAUGE
YIELD: 4 PINTS

4 pounds fresh tomatillos, papery husks removed, washed and quartered

¼ cup freshly squeezed lemon juice (from about 2 lemons)

1. Prepare 4 pint jars and the canner: Clean the jars and prepare the 2-piece lids according to the manufacturer's guidelines. Keep the jars in hot but not boiling water until you're ready to use them. Prepare the canner by filling it with 2 to 3 inches of water and bringing it to a simmer, or according to your manufacturer's directions.

2. In large pot, combine the tomatillos with enough water to cover. Bring to boil over high heat and boil for 5 to 10 minutes until tender.

3. With a large spoon, carefully fill the jars with the tomatillos and some cooking water, leaving ½ inch of headspace.

4. Add 1 tablespoon of lemon juice to each jar.

5. Remove air bubbles with a plastic or wooden utensil, adding more hot liquid as needed to maintain the proper ½-inch headspace.

6. Wipe the rims and seal the jars hand-tight with the 2-piece lids.

7. Carefully transfer the filled jars to the rack inside the pressure canner. Process the jars at the pressure listed above for 10 minutes.

8. Let the canner return to 0 pounds pressure. Wait 10 minutes more, then carefully open the canner lid according to the manufacturer's instructions.

9. With a jar lifter, remove the jars and place them on a clean dishtowel away from any drafts. Once the jars cool to room temperature, check the seals. If any jars have not sealed, refrigerate them and use the tomatillos within 2 weeks. Label the remaining jars with the recipe name and date before storing.

PINEAPPLE-FLAVORED ZUCCHINI

Zucchini is one of those vegetables that can quickly overwhelm you with a bumper crop. Some years my garden produces so many zucchini I don't know what I'd do if I couldn't can them. With that large quantity in mind, I'm always looking for new flavors to break the zucchini monotony. This one might sound wacky, but try it before you write it off. Fresh zucchini has a mild flavor that I've found takes on the flavor of its canning liquid more than other vegetables. Using pineapple juice with a hint of lemon creates a tropical twist the whole family will love. Shredding the zucchini increases the surface area to soak up as much pineapple goodness as possible.

PROCESSING TIME: 25 MINUTES | **PRESSURE: 10 POUNDS WEIGHTED GAUGE, 11 POUNDS DIAL GAUGE**
YIELD: 6 PINTS

9 cups shredded
zucchini

3 cups sugar

5¾ cups (46 ounces)
canned pineapple juice

½ cup freshly squeezed
lemon juice (from about
4 lemons)

1. Prepare 6 pint jars and the canner: Clean the jars and prepare the 2-piece lids according to the manufacturer's guidelines. Keep the jars in hot but not boiling water until you're ready to use them. Prepare the canner by filling it with 2 to 3 inches of water and bringing it to a simmer, or according to your manufacturer's directions.

2. In a large pot over medium-high heat, combine the zucchini, sugar, pineapple juice, and lemon juice. Bring to a simmer and cook and for 20 minutes.

3. With a large spoon, carefully pack the zucchini into the hot jars, dividing it and the juice evenly among the jars, leaving ½ inch of headspace.

4. Remove air bubbles with a plastic or wooden utensil, adding hot juice as needed to maintain the proper ½-inch headspace.

5. Wipe the rims and seal the jars hand-tight with the 2-piece lids.

6. Carefully transfer the filled jars to the rack inside the pressure canner. Process the jars at the pressure listed above for 25 minutes.

7. Let the canner return to 0 pounds pressure. Wait 10 minutes more, then carefully open the canner lid according to the manufacturer's instructions.

8. With a jar lifter, remove the jars and place them on a clean dishtowel away from any drafts. Once the jars cool to room temperature, check the seals. If any jars have not sealed, refrigerate them and use the zucchini within 2 weeks. Label the remaining jars with the recipe name and date before storing.

SWEET AND SPICY PICKLED BRUSSELS SPROUTS

From kimchi to sauerkraut, cabbage is one of the most popular pickling vegetables the world over. Brussels sprouts are a fellow member of the brassica family, and, while their flavor is unique, there's no denying they share a certain something with cabbage. So, for this recipe I let them shine in a pickle. Simply halving them creates perfect bite-size morsels; of course, you can break them down further by dicing them after pickling. I recommend letting these sit at least 2 weeks in the jar after pickling to develop the proper amount of flavor.

PROCESSING TIME: 10 MINUTES | PRESSURE: 10 POUNDS WEIGHTED GAUGE, 11 POUNDS DIAL GAUGE
YIELD: 5 PINTS

2 pounds brussels sprouts, washed, trimmed, brown leaves discarded, and halved

10 tablespoons canning salt, divided

5 garlic cloves, peeled

5 cups distilled white vinegar

5 cups water

1½ teaspoons red pepper flakes

1. Prepare 5 pint jars and the canner: Clean the jars and prepare the 2-piece lids according to the manufacturer's guidelines. Keep the jars in hot but not boiling water until you're ready to use them. Prepare the canner by filling it with 2 to 3 inches of water and bringing it to a simmer, or according to your manufacturer's directions.

2. Soak the brussels sprouts in a large bowl of lightly salted water (3 tablespoons of salt) for 20 minutes. Drain well.

3. Evenly divide the sprouts among the jars, leaving ¾ inch of headspace. Add 1 garlic clove to each jar.

4. In a large pot over high heat, combine the vinegar, water, remaining canning salt, and red pepper flakes. Bring to a boil and stir until the salt dissolves completely.

5. Carefully ladle the hot pickling liquid into each jar, leaving ½ inch of headspace.

6. Remove air bubbles with a plastic or wooden utensil, adding more hot liquid as needed to maintain the proper ½-inch headspace.

7. Wipe the rims and seal the jars hand-tight with the 2-piece lids.

8. Carefully transfer the filled jars to the rack inside the pressure canner. Process the jars at the pressure listed above for 10 minutes.

9. Let the canner return to 0 pounds pressure. Wait 10 minutes more, then carefully open the canner lid according to the manufacturer's instructions.

10. With a jar lifter, remove the jars and place them on a clean dishtowel away from any drafts. Once the jars cool to room temperature, check the seals. If any jars have not sealed, refrigerate them and use the brussels sprouts within 2 weeks. Label the remaining jars with the recipe name and date before storing.

RAINBOW PEPPERS

We eat first with our eyes, and this recipe is one of the best for adding a pop of color to your mid-winter recipes. That said, my family also loves these in summer. We'll often grill sausages and top them with sautéed onions and these peppers. It's like the best of the county fair brought home—only tastier. As an added bonus, you'll feel healthier the next day as you won't be eating those funnel cakes for dessert.

PROCESSING TIME: 35 MINUTES | PRESSURE: 10 POUNDS WEIGHTED GAUGE, 11 POUNDS DIAL GAUGE
YIELD: 5 PINTS

2 quarts water

5 pounds assorted bell peppers, any color, washed, quartered, stemmed, and seeded

5 tablespoons freshly squeezed lemon juice (from about 3 lemons)

2½ teaspoons canning salt

1. Prepare 5 pint jars and the canner: Clean the jars and prepare the 2-piece lids according to the manufacturer's guidelines. Keep the jars in hot but not boiling water until you're ready to use them. Prepare the canner by filling it with 2 to 3 inches of water and bringing it to a simmer, or according to your manufacturer's directions.

2. In a medium-size pot over high heat, bring the water to a boil.

3. Pack the peppers into the hot jars as firmly as possible.

4. Carefully pour or ladle the boiling water over the peppers, leaving 1 inch of headspace in the jars.

5. Add 1 tablespoon of lemon juice and ½ teaspoon of canning salt to each jar.

6. Remove air bubbles with a plastic or wooden utensil, adding more boiling water as needed to maintain the proper 1-inch headspace.

7. Wipe the rims and seal the jars hand-tight with the 2-piece lids.

8. Carefully transfer the filled jars to the rack inside the pressure canner. Process the jars at the pressure listed above for 35 minutes.

9. Let the canner return to 0 pounds pressure. Wait 10 minutes more, then carefully open the canner lid according to the manufacturer's instructions.

10. With a jar lifter, remove the jars and place them on a clean dishtowel away from any drafts. Once the jars cool to room temperature, check the seals. If any jars have not sealed, refrigerate them and use the peppers within 2 weeks. Label the remaining jars with the recipe name and date before storing.

VEGETABLE SOUP

It's a mystery to me why many children who avoid vegetables come dinnertime will eat a full bowl of vegetable soup. Who am I to argue? I'm always happy to find a way to make sure my kids eat the vegetables I put in front of them. This soup is a personal favorite. It's what I reach for to pack a thermos for lunch when I'm headed out for the day. It's hearty and filling on its own, but you can make it more of a meal with a thick slice of buttered bread. One important note: make sure you use chickpeas or another bean that has been precooked—don't use dried beans in this recipe!

PROCESSING TIME: 1 HOUR | **PRESSURE: 10 POUNDS WEIGHTED GAUGE, 11 POUNDS DIAL GAUGE**
YIELD: 3 PINTS

1 pint canned tomatoes

2 cups water

1 cup canned corn

1 cup canned and drained chickpeas, or other cooked bean

3 carrots, sliced

1½ pounds potatoes, peeled and cubed

1 medium-size onion, chopped

½ cup chopped celery

2 garlic cloves, minced

Salt and pepper to taste

1 teaspoon dried Italian seasoning

1. Prepare 3 pint jars and the canner: Clean the jars and prepare the 2-piece lids according to the manufacturer's guidelines. Keep the jars in hot but not boiling water until you're ready to use them. Prepare the canner by filling it with 2 to 3 inches of water and bringing it to a simmer, or according to your manufacturer's directions.

2. In a large heavy stockpot over high heat, combine the tomatoes, water, corn, chickpeas, carrots, potatoes, onion, celery, and garlic. Season with salt and pepper. Stir to combine and bring to a boil. Reduce the heat to a simmer and stir in the Italian seasoning. Simmer the soup for 10 minutes.

3. Increase the heat and bring the soup to a boil again.

4. Carefully ladle the hot soup into the hot jars, leaving 1 inch of headspace.

5. Remove air bubbles with a plastic or wooden utensil, adding more hot soup as needed to maintain the proper 1-inch headspace.

6. Wipe the rims and seal the jars hand-tight with the 2-piece lids.

7. Carefully transfer the filled jars to the rack inside the pressure canner. Process the jars at the pressure listed above for 1 hour.

8. Let the canner return to 0 pounds pressure. Wait 10 minutes more, then carefully open the canner lid according to the manufacturer's instructions.

9. With a jar lifter, remove the jars and place them on a clean dishtowel away from any drafts. Once the jars cool to room temperature, check the seals. If any jars have not sealed, refrigerate them and use the soup within 2 weeks. Label the remaining jars with the recipe name and date before storing.

CHAPTER FIVE

PRESSURE CANNING FRUITS

FRUITS ARE ONE OF THE MOST REWARDING FOODS TO CAN if you love sharing food with family and friends. Everyone loves a sweet treat, whether it's meant to be spread on warm bread, spooned over ice cream, or nibbled as part of an appetizer spread. Unlike canned vegetables, store-bought jams, jellies, and even canned fruit don't have a bad reputation. So why can? Because you can take good to great! And you get the same benefits as canning your vegetables: You know how your food was grown and every ingredient that goes into the jar.

I also enjoy canning fruits because they are precious. Our seasons in northern Maine are very short, so preserving as much as possible means my family can eat a lot more peaches and blueberry pie than we could if limited to the few weeks when the produce is locally available. Canned fruits are also beautiful. It's rewarding to look at a shelf overflowing with peaches, and who doesn't smile when given a jar of freshly canned berries?

As you get going, you'll notice a few differences between home-canned fruit and store-bought. For one, home-canned food doesn't look like factory-canned food—and that's okay. No matter how particular you are at home, perfection is not always picture perfect. Even when your fruits and vegetables are ripe, tasty, and nutritious, at times they are not the same size, shape, and color that is the industry standard. Yet, this doesn't stop canned fruit from being beautiful. The colors are simply wonderful and a cupboard full of colorful glass jars beats metal cans any day.

SUGAR SYRUP

There are five options for sugar syrup, named according to the amount of sugar in the water. Even when a recipe calls for one type of syrup, you can use a different syrup if you know your family likes sweeter (or less sweet) results. Swapping out sugar syrups is one of the few dramatic changes you can make to these recipes without affecting food safety. Most recipes will tell you to add hot syrup to the jars, so making a syrup ahead of time and refrigerating it will not speed up anything the day you can.

To make any of these syrups, dissolve the sugar in the water as part of the canning process.

Very light sugar syrup: 4 cups water to ½ cup sugar

Light sugar syrup: 4 cups water to 1 cup sugar

Medium sugar syrup: 4 cups water to 2 cups sugar

Heavy sugar syrup: 4 cups water to 3 cups sugar

Very heavy sugar syrup: 4 cups water to 4 cups sugar

Home canning will bring a new appreciation for the actual taste of fruit as well. If you have ever looked on the back of a jar of canned fruit, you can see that there is a laundry list of extra ingredients you certainly never put into your own homemade fruit—thickeners, high fructose corn syrup, salt, the list goes on. In fact, there is no reason even to add heavy sugar syrup to your canned fruits. There are, in fact, many levels of sugar syrups (see above), and the end product is still delicious. (Even if you do prefer a heavy syrup, when you make it yourself, you know it's made from pure cane sugar and water, not high fructose corn syrup.)

APPLE PIE FILLING

You might think that apple pie filling would simply be Canned Apples (page 117) with the addition of apple pie spices. While it's true that apples meant for pie should be spiced when canned, there are a couple of other key differences. First, we'll use sugar and Clear Jel instead of a sugar syrup. This helps you get the consistency you want for a pie filling. Second, a hint of lemon juice is added as well. Don't worry, this won't make for a tart apple pie. It helps balance the sweetness and creates a better-quality pie filling. In addition to baking these apples into a classic apple pie, try them in hand pies, cobbler, and filled sweet bread, to name a few.

PROCESSING TIME: 10 MINUTES | PRESSURE: 10 POUNDS WEIGHTED GAUGE, 11 POUNDS DIAL GAUGE
YIELD: 4 PINTS

6 pounds apples, washed, cored, peeled, and sliced or cubed into even bite-size pieces

2 cups sugar

½ cup Clear Jel

2 tablespoons freshly squeezed lemon juice (from about 1 lemon)

2 teaspoons ground cinnamon

½ teaspoon ground nutmeg

1. Prepare 4 pint jars and the canner: Clean the jars and prepare the 2-piece lids according to the manufacturer's guidelines. Keep the jars in hot but not boiling water until you're ready to use them. Prepare the canner by filling it with 2 to 3 inches of water and bringing it to a simmer, or according to your manufacturer's directions.

2. In a large pot over medium heat, combine the apples, sugar, Clear Jel, lemon juice, cinnamon, and nutmeg. Cook until just thickened.

3. Pack the hot jars with the apple pieces and pour the thickened syrup over them, leaving ½ inch of headspace.

4. Remove any air bubbles with a plastic or wooden utensil, adding more hot syrup as needed to maintain the proper ½-inch headspace.

5. Wipe the rims and seal the jars hand-tight with the 2-piece lids.

6. Carefully transfer the filled jars to the rack inside the pressure canner. Process the jars at the pressure listed above for 10 minutes.

7. Let the canner return to 0 pounds pressure. Wait 10 minutes more, then carefully open the canner lid according to the manufacturer's instructions.

8. With a jar lifter, remove the jars and place them on a clean dishtowel away from any drafts. One the jars cool to room temperature, check the seals. If any jars have not sealed, refrigerate them and use the filling within 1 week. Label the remaining jars with the recipe name and date before storing.

CANNED APPLES

We have apple trees in our yard, so I always begin my canned apple recipe by tasting our fresh apples. From there, I know if I want to adjust the taste by mixing them with another type of apple, and also which sugar syrup I want to use. Serve your canned apples warmed, over ice cream, or crush some graham crackers for an impromptu "crust" and top with freshly whipped cream. A (canned) apple a day keeps the doctor away!

PROCESSING TIME: 10 MINUTES | PRESSURE: 5 POUNDS WEIGHTED GAUGE, 6 POUNDS DIAL GAUGE
YIELD: 4 PINTS

6 pounds apples, washed, cored, peeled, and sliced into uniform, bite-size pieces

1 recipe sugar syrup of choice (page 114), at a boil

1. Prepare 4 pint jars and the canner: Clean the jars and prepare the 2-piece lids according to the manufacturer's guidelines. Keep the jars in hot but not boiling water until you're ready to use them. Prepare the canner by filling it with 2 to 3 inches of water and bringing it to a simmer, or according to your manufacturer's directions.

2. Pack your hot jars with apple pieces.

3. Carefully pour or ladle the hot syrup over the apples, leaving ½ inch of headspace.

4. Remove air bubbles with a plastic or wooden utensil, adding more hot syrup as needed to maintain the proper ½-inch headspace.

5. Wipe the rims and seal the jars hand-tight with the 2-piece lids.

6. Carefully transfer the filled jars to the rack inside the pressure canner. Process the jars at the pressure listed above for 10 minutes.

7. Let the canner return to 0 pounds pressure. Wait 10 minutes more, then carefully open the canner lid according to the manufacturer's instructions.

8. With a jar lifter, remove the jars and place them on a clean dishtowel away from any drafts. Once the jars cool to room temperature, check the seals. If any jars have not sealed, refrigerate them and use the apples within 1 week. Label the remaining jars with the recipe name and date before storing.

APPLESAUCE

Apples are positively a delight for canners. They can be canned as sliced fruit, for pie filling, or applesauce—and I've included recipes for all three in this chapter. Part of the secret to the best apple recipes is figuring out what apples you and your family like best. It's generally more interesting to use a mix of apples—some sweeter and some more tart—when you make applesauce. The other thing to consider is the season. While summer apples aren't typically good for canning as sliced fruit, they actually make applesauce that's quite good. They are sweet and cook down quickly, and I've found they tend to produce a silky smooth sauce.

PROCESSING TIME: 10 MINUTES | **PRESSURE: 5 POUNDS WEIGHTED GAUGE, 6 POUNDS DIAL GAUGE**
YIELD: 4 PINTS

6 pounds apples, washed, cored, peeled, and halved

Cinnamon to taste

1 recipe sugar syrup of choice (page 114), at a boil

1. Prepare 4 pint jars and the canner: Clean the jars and prepare the 2-piece lids according to the manufacturer's guidelines. Keep the jars in hot but not boiling water until you're ready to use them. Prepare the canner by filling it with 2 to 3 inches of water and bringing it to a simmer, or according to your manufacturer's directions.

2. In a large, heavy pot over medium heat, combine the apples and cinnamon, as desired. Cook the apples until very soft, stirring occasionally.

3. Carefully pack the jars with the hot apples.

4. Carefully pour or ladle the hot syrup over the apples, leaving ½ inch of headspace.

5. Remove any air bubbles with a plastic or wooden utensil, adding more hot syrup as needed to maintain the proper ½-inch headspace.

6. Wipe the rims and seal the jars hand-tight with the 2-piece lids.

7. Carefully transfer the filled jars to the rack inside the pressure canner. Process the jars at the pressure listed above for 10 minutes.

8. Let the canner return to 0 pounds pressure. Wait 10 minutes more, then carefully open the canner lid according to the manufacturer's instructions.

9. With a jar lifter, remove the jars and place them on a clean dishtowel away from any drafts. Once the jars cool to room temperature, check the seals. If any jars have not sealed, refrigerate them and use the applesauce within 1 week. Label the remaining jars with the recipe name and date before storing.

BLUEBERRY FILLING

Here in Maine a freezer full of wild blueberries is considered normal. Our growing seasons may be short, but they can be bountiful! In my family, we celebrate these tasty berries by eating them in every conceivable way—including straight from the freezer. Of course, I also can some so we'll have luscious pie filling on hand when the season is over. Use this filling to make pies, cobblers, buckles, and tarts, and spoon it over ice cream and yogurt. While this recipe isn't meant to be as thick as a store-bought can of blueberry filling, it will be much more flavorful.

**PROCESSING TIME: 10 MINUTES | PRESSURE: 10 POUNDS WEIGHTED GAUGE, 11 POUNDS DIAL GAUGE
YIELD: 2 PINTS**

¾ cup sugar

1 cup water

¼ cup Clear Jel

3½ teaspoons freshly squeezed lemon juice (from about 1 lemon)

3½ cups fresh or frozen and thawed blueberries

1. Prepare 2 pint jars and the canner: Clean the jars and prepare the 2-piece lids according to the manufacturer's guidelines. Keep the jars in hot but not boiling water until you're ready to use them. Prepare the canner by filling it with 2 to 3 inches of water and bringing it to a simmer, or according to your manufacturer's directions.

2. In a medium-size saucepan over medium-high heat, combine the sugar, water, and Clear Jel. Cook until the mixture thickens.

3. Stir in the lemon juice and boil for 1 minute, stirring constantly so the mixture doesn't burn.

4. Carefully fold in the blueberries and immediately pack the hot mixture into the hot jars, leaving 1 inch of headspace.

5. Remove any air bubbles with a plastic or wooden utensil, adding more blueberries and hot liquid as needed to maintain the proper 1-inch headspace.

6. Wipe the rims and seal the jars hand-tight with the 2-piece lids.

7. Carefully transfer the filled jars to the rack inside the pressure canner. Process the jars at the pressure listed above for 10 minutes.

8. Let the canner return to 0 pounds pressure. Wait 10 minutes more, then carefully open the canner lid according to the manufacturer's instructions.

9. With a jar lifter, remove the jars and place them on a clean dishtowel away from any drafts. Once the jars cool to room temperature, check the seals. If any jars have not sealed, refrigerate them and use the filling within 1 week. Label the remaining jars with the recipe name and date before storing.

RHUBARB FILLING

Rhubarb used to be an underrated fruit—farmers practically gave it away! However, that has changed in the past decade as people were drawn to its showstopping looks and unique flavor. Since rhubarb contains a decent amount of water, I like to unlock the fruit's moisture to can instead of adding water to the recipe. While adding water is certainly the faster way to can, it results in canned rhubarb with a fraction of the flavor. Instead, just allow the ingredients to sit for 4 hours before you can them. Once you try a bite you'll agree the wait is worth it.

PROCESSING TIME: 10 MINUTES | PRESSURE: 10 POUNDS WEIGHTED GAUGE, 11 POUNDS DIAL GAUGE
YIELD: 6 PINTS

6 pounds rhubarb, leaves removed, sliced into ½-inch pieces

3 cups sugar

1. In a large pot, combine the rhubarb pieces and sugar and stir well to combine. Let stand for 4 hours, so the rhubarb can create its own juice.

2. Meanwhile, prepare 6 pint jars and the canner: Clean the jars and prepare the 2-piece lids according to the manufacturer's guidelines. Keep the jars in hot but not boiling water until you're ready to use them. Prepare the canner by filling it with 2 to 3 inches of water and bringing it to a simmer, or according to your manufacturer's directions.

3. After the 4 hours is up, bring the rhubarb and sugar mixture to a boil over medium-high heat. Stir well to prevent any sticking.

4. Carefully pack the rhubarb and hot syrup into the hot jars, leaving 1 inch of headspace.

5. Remove any air bubbles with a plastic or wooden utensil, adding more hot syrup as needed to maintain the proper 1-inch headspace.

6. Wipe the rims and seal the jars hand-tight with the 2-piece lids.

7. Carefully transfer the filled jars to the rack inside the pressure canner. Process the jars at the pressure listed above for 10 minutes.

8. Let the canner return to 0 pounds pressure. Wait 10 minutes more, then carefully open the canner lid according to the manufacturer's instructions.

9. With a jar lifter, remove the jars and place them on a clean dishtowel away from any drafts. Once the jars cool to room temperature, check the seals. If any jars have not sealed, refrigerate them and use the filling within 1 week. Label the remaining jars with the recipe name and date before storing.

RHUBARB SAUCE

If your family can't get enough rhubarb, or if rhubarb is particularly abundant in your neck of the woods, try this unique preparation. Note that rhubarb sauce is not a topping for ice cream or other desserts (though I suppose you could use it that way). It's actually a spin on applesauce! Sure, in its raw form, rhubarb doesn't taste a lot like apples, but once you cook it, it shares that addictive sweet/ tart balance of a good Granny Smith. Take a step off the beaten path and try this rhubarb sauce.

PROCESSING TIME: 10 MINUTES | PRESSURE: 10 POUNDS WEIGHTED GAUGE, 11 POUNDS DIAL GAUGE
YIELD: 4 PINTS

4 pounds rhubarb, leaves and white end removed and discarded, red and green stem parts chopped into ¼-inch pieces

4 cups sugar

1. Prepare 4 pint jars and the canner: Clean the jars and prepare the 2-piece lids according to the manufacturer's guidelines. Keep the jars in hot but not boiling water until you're ready to use them. Prepare the canner by filling it with 2 to 3 inches of water and bringing it to a simmer, or according to your manufacturer's directions.

2. In a large pot over medium-high heat, combine the rhubarb pieces and sugar. Cook until it becomes a thick sauce, stirring often to prevent burning, about 30 minutes.

3. Carefully ladle the boiling-hot sauce into the hot jars, leaving 1 inch of headspace.

4. Remove any air bubbles with a plastic or wooden utensil, adding more hot sauce as needed to maintain the proper 1-inch headspace.

5. Wipe the rims and seal the jars hand-tight with the 2-piece lids.

6. Carefully transfer the filled jars to the rack inside the pressure canner Process the jars at the pressure listed above for 10 minutes.

7. Let the canner return to 0 pounds pressure. Wait 10 minutes more, then carefully open the canner lid according to the manufacturer's instructions.

8. With a jar lifter, remove the jars and place them on a clean dishtowel away from any drafts. Once the jars cool to room temperature, check the seals. If any jars have not sealed, refrigerate them and use the sauce within 1 week. Label the remaining jars with the recipe name and date before storing.

SPICED PEARS

When my family lived in Nebraska, there was a huge mature pear tree in our yard. With more pears than we could eat, I learned to make spiced pears and have included them in my summer canning repertoire ever since. These are lightly seasoned, so the true pear flavor shines through. My biggest piece of advice, besides using delicious ripe pears, is to use fresh spices as well. An aromatic cinnamon stick and vanilla bean are what you want here—not one languishing for months (or years) in the pantry.

PROCESSING TIME: 11 MINUTES | PRESSURE: 5 POUNDS WEIGHTED GAUGE, 6 POUNDS DIAL GAUGE
YIELD: 3 PINTS

6 cups water, divided

2 tablespoons Fruit-Fresh

3 pounds pears, peeled, cored, and quartered (see step 2)

1 cup sugar

1 cinnamon stick

½ vanilla bean, split widthwise

1. Prepare 3 pint jars and the canner: Clean the jars and prepare the 2-piece lids according to the manufacturer's guidelines. Keep the jars in hot but not boiling water until you're ready to use them. Prepare the canner by filling it with 2 to 3 inches of water and bringing it to a simmer, or according to your manufacturer's directions.

2. In a large bowl, mix together 2 cups of water and the Fruit-Fresh. Immediately place the pears as they're cut in the bowl. This helps keep them from browning.

3. In a large pot over medium-high heat, combine the remaining 4 cups of water, the sugar, cinnamon stick, and vanilla bean quarters. Bring the mixture to a boil.

4. Drain the pears and add them to the pot. Return the mixture to a boil and cook for 5 minutes. Remove and discard the vanilla bean.

5. Carefully ladle the boiling-hot pears and liquid into the hot jars, leaving ½ inch of headspace.

6. Remove any air bubbles with a plastic or wooden utensil, adding more hot liquid as needed to maintain the proper ½-inch headspace.

7. Wipe the rims and seal the jars hand-tight with the 2-piece lids.

8. Carefully transfer the filled jars to the rack inside the pressure canner. Process the jars at the pressure listed above for 11 minutes.

9. Let the canner return to 0 pounds pressure. Wait 10 minutes more, then carefully open the canner lid according to the manufacturer's instructions.

10. With a jar lifter, remove the jars and place them on a clean dishtowel away from any drafts. Once the jars cool to room temperature, check the seals. If any jars have not sealed, refrigerate them and use the pears within 1 week. Label the remaining jars with the recipe name and date before storing.

CANNED CHERRIES

When I was a child growing up in upstate New York, our family went cherry picking most every year. Picking the flats of cherries was great fun, but pitting all those cherries was a nightmare. My mother made the work worth it by canning plenty of fresh cherries, which we enjoyed throughout the year. Cherries have such a short season in most parts of the country; you just need to can or freeze them if you love this fruit. These days, even with the invention of the cherry pitter, I tend to stick to one flat of cherries. Their appearance on the table from time to time is a special treat.

**PROCESSING TIME: 8 MINUTES | PRESSURE: 5 POUNDS WEIGHTED GAUGE, 6 POUNDS DIAL GAUGE
YIELD: 4 PINTS**

1 cup sugar

7 cups water

6 pounds pitted cherries

1. Prepare 4 pint jars and the canner: Clean the jars and prepare the 2-piece lids according to the manufacturer's guidelines. Keep the jars in hot but not boiling water until you're ready to use them. Prepare the canner by filling it with 2 to 3 inches of water and bringing it to a simmer, or according to your manufacturer's directions.

2. In a large pot over medium-high heat, combine the sugar and water. Heat, stirring, until the sugar dissolves completely.

3. Add the pitted cherries to the hot sugar syrup. Return the mixture to a boil and cook for 5 minutes.

4. Carefully ladle the hot cherries and syrup into the hot jars, leaving ½ inch of headspace.

5. Remove any air bubbles with a plastic or wooden utensil, adding more hot syrup as needed to maintain the proper ½-inch headspace.

6. Wipe the rims and seal the jars hand-tight with the 2-piece lids.

7. Carefully transfer the filled jars to the rack inside the pressure canner. Process the jars at the pressure listed above for 8 minutes.

8. Let the canner return to 0 pounds pressure. Wait 10 minutes more, then carefully open the canner lid according to the manufacturer's instructions.

9. With a jar lifter, remove the jars and place them on a clean dishtowel away from any drafts. Once the jars cool to room temperature, check the seals. If any jars have not sealed, refrigerate them and use the cherries within 1 week. Label the remaining jars with the recipe name and date before storing.

CANNED PEACHES

Of all the canned fruits, peaches are one of the most drastically different between homemade and store-bought. (While you might find tasty applesauce at the grocery store, good luck finding canned peaches you truly enjoy!) While most people think of them as a summery fruit, add the right spices to dishes like spiced peach cobbler and there's no arguing it's meant for eating fireside.

PROCESSING TIME: 10 MINUTES | **PRESSURE: 5 POUNDS WEIGHTED GAUGE, 6 POUNDS DIAL GAUGE**
YIELD: 4 PINTS

3 pounds ripe peaches

3 cups water

¾ cup sugar

1. Prepare 4 pint jars and the canner: Clean the jars and prepare the 2-piece lids according to the manufacturer's guidelines. Keep the jars in hot but not boiling water until you're ready to use them. Prepare the canner by filling it with 2 to 3 inches of water and bringing it to a simmer, or according to your manufacturer's directions.

2. Bring a medium-size pot of water to a boil and prepare a separate ice-water bath in a large bowl. This is to help remove the skins from the peaches—the 3 cups of water listed above is for the recipe.

3. Remove the peach skins: One at a time, place the peaches into the boiling water for 30 seconds. With tongs or a slotted spoon, remove the peach and place it into the bowl of ice water. The peels should come off easily. Repeat with the remaining peaches. Cut the peeled peaches into uniform slices.

4. In a large pot over medium-high heat, combine the 3 cups of water and sugar. Bring to a boil, stirring until the sugar dissolves completely.

5. Add the peaches and return the mixture to a boil.

6. Carefully ladle the hot peaches and syrup liquid into hot jars, leaving ½ inch of headspace.

7. Remove any air bubbles with a plastic or wooden utensil, adding more hot syrup as needed to maintain the proper ½-inch headspace.

8. Wipe the rims and seal the jars hand-tight with the 2-piece lids.

9. Carefully transfer the filled jars to the rack inside the pressure canner. Process the jars at the pressure listed above for 10 minutes.

10. Let the canner return to 0 pounds pressure. Wait 10 minutes more, then carefully open the canner lid according to the manufacturer's instructions.

11. With a jar lifter, remove the jars and place them on a clean dishtowel away from any drafts. Once the jars cool to room temperature, check the seals. If any jars have not sealed, refrigerate them and use the peaches within 1 week. Label the remaining jars with the recipe name and date before storing.

WHOLE CRANBERRIES

Cranberries aren't a local fruit for most of the country but they sure are here in Maine. We know the owners of the nearby cranberry bogs, and perhaps that makes them taste even better. Cranberries travel well and are easy to find nationwide around Thanksgiving. You can freeze them until you have time to use them, too. I've found there isn't much difference between canning fresh or frozen cranberries. This recipe is designed to be sweet, but not so sweet it completely hides the tartness of the cranberries. Serve it next Thanksgiving topped with fresh orange zest or spread it on a turkey sandwich any time of year.

PROCESSING TIME: 30 MINUTES | PRESSURE: 5 POUNDS WEIGHTED GAUGE, 6 POUNDS DIAL GAUGE YIELD: 2 PINTS

2 cups water

2 cups sugar

4 cups fresh whole cranberries

1. Prepare 2 pint jars and the canner: Clean the jars and prepare the 2-piece lids according to the manufacturer's guidelines. Keep the jars in hot but not boiling water until you're ready to use them. Prepare the canner by filling it with 2 to 3 inches of water and bringing it to a simmer, or according to your manufacturer's directions.

2. In a large pot over medium-high heat, combine the water and sugar. Bring to a boil, stirring, until the sugar dissolves completely.

3. Fill the hot jars with the raw cranberries, leaving 1 inch of headspace.

4. Once the boiling-hot syrup is ready, carefully ladle it over the cranberries in the jars, leaving ½ inch of headspace.

5. Remove any air bubbles with a plastic or wooden utensil, adding more hot syrup as needed to maintain the proper ½-inch headspace.

6. Wipe the rims and seal the jars hand-tight with the 2-piece lids.

7. Carefully transfer the filled jars to the rack inside the pressure canner. Process the jars at the pressure listed above for 30 minutes.

8. Let the canner return to 0 pounds pressure. Wait 10 minutes more, then carefully open the canner lid according to the manufacturer's instructions.

9. With a jar lifter, remove the jars and place them on a clean dishtowel away from any drafts. Once the jars cool to room temperature, check the seals. If any jars have not sealed, refrigerate them and use the cranberries within 1 week. Label the remaining jars with the recipe name and date before storing.

CRANBERRY JELLY

Every family is different, but, given the choice, my family is a cranberry jelly crowd through and through. You can keep the chunky sauce—pass us the jelly! In fact, I've often wondered why cranberry jelly isn't available year-round. It makes the perfect condiment to many a dish, and my kids will eat it like a treat. Sure, there's sugar involved, but at least there's some fruit—unlike that chocolate pudding or peanut butter ice cream.

PROCESSING TIME: 10 MINUTES | PRESSURE: 5 POUNDS WEIGHTED GAUGE, 6 POUNDS DIAL GAUGE
YIELD: 2 PINTS

4 cups fresh whole cranberries

2 cups sugar

Finely chopped peel of 1 orange

Juice of 1 orange plus enough water to equal 1 cup liquid

1 cinnamon stick

1. Prepare 2 pint jars and the canner: Clean the jars and prepare the 2-piece lids according to the manufacturer's guidelines. Keep the jars in hot but not boiling water until you're ready to use them. Prepare the canner by filling it with 2 to 3 inches of water and bringing it to a simmer, or according to your manufacturer's directions.

2. In a large pot over medium-high heat (the mixture will foam, so use a larger pot than you think you need), combine the cranberries, sugar, orange peel, orange juice plus water, and cinnamon stick. Cook the mixture until it cooks down just a bit, about 10 minutes.

3. Strain the cranberry mixture through a fine-mesh sieve into a smaller pot, pressing on the berries to remove as much cranberry liquid from the stems, seeds, and peelings as possible. Discard the solids.

4. Bring the strained liquid back to a boil over medium-high heat.

5. Carefully ladle the hot cranberry liquid into the hot jars, leaving ½ inch of headspace.

6. Remove any air bubbles with a plastic or wooden utensil, topping off the jars as needed to maintain the proper ½-inch headspace.

7. Wipe the rims and seal the jars hand-tight with the 2-piece lids.

8. Carefully transfer the filled jars to the rack inside the pressure canner. Process the jars at the pressure listed above for 10 minutes.

9. Let the canner return to 0 pounds pressure. Wait 10 minutes more, then carefully open the canner lid according to the manufacturer's instructions.

10. With a jar lifter, remove the jars and place them on a clean dishtowel away from any drafts. Once the jars cool to room temperature, check the seals. If any jars have not sealed, refrigerate them and use the jelly within 1 week. Label the remaining jars with the recipe name and date before storing.

HOMEMADE GRAPE DRINK

I think this is one of the best recipes in the whole book, and it is fun for the entire family. Have you ever tried wild grapes? On our farm, they grow taller than our house and line the entire back of the yard. All summer long, we check and recheck the fruits until after the first frost, when the grapes suddenly go from super tart to sweet, juicy treats. Canning juice is the best way to keep that lovely flavor. Try this recipe with any sweet, juicy grapes you can get your hands on. While this recipe does have a good amount of sugar, you are making a concentrate that tastes better and is, at least, slightly more wholesome than those powdered drink mixes. To use this concentrate, pour the canned juice and grapes from one jar into a mesh strainer, catching the juice in a 1-quart container. Discard the grapes. Add enough cold water to make a full quart. Serve over ice and enjoy!

PROCESSING TIME: 10 MINUTES | PRESSURE: 10 POUNDS WEIGHTED GAUGE, 11 POUNDS DIAL GAUGE
YIELD: 2 PINTS

---

3 cups grapes, rinsed

1¼ cups sugar

1. Prepare 2 pint jars and the canner: Clean the jars and prepare the 2-piece lids according to the manufacturer's guidelines. Keep the jars in hot but not boiling water until you're ready to use them. Prepare the canner by filling it with 2 to 3 inches of water and bringing it to a simmer, or according to your manufacturer's directions.

2. Evenly divide the grapes between the 2 hot jars.

3. In a 2-cup (or larger) glass measuring cup, add the sugar and top it off with hot water until it reaches the 2-cup mark. Microwave on high power for a minute or two depending on your microwave's power, and stir until the sugar dissolves. Pour the sugar water over the grapes, leaving 1 inch of headspace.

4. Remove any air bubbles with a plastic or wooden utensil, adding more hot sugar water as needed to maintain the proper 1-inch headspace.

5. Wipe the rims and seal the jars hand-tight with the 2-piece lids.

6. Carefully transfer the filled jars to the rack inside the pressure canner. Process the jars at the pressure listed above for 10 minutes.

7. Let the canner return to 0 pounds pressure. Wait 10 minutes more, then carefully open the canner lid according to the manufacturer's instructions.

8. With a jar lifter, remove the jars and place them on a clean dishtowel away from any drafts. Once the jars cool to room temperature, check the seals. If any jars have not sealed, refrigerate them and use the juice within 2 weeks.

CHAPTER SIX

PRESSURE CANNING MEAT

We raise our own meat here on the farm, so we know just how precious and valuable meat truly is. These days, I endeavor to make meat more of a supporting character in recipes than the main star. Yet reducing the amount of meat you eat makes it even more important that the meat you use is of the best quality and flavor.

The same goes when buying meat. More of us than ever are paying attention to where our meat comes from, asking important questions of our producers. How were the animals raised? What were they fed? The answers have a very real impact on the quality of the meat you buy.

Since meat tends to be the most expensive item on any grocery list, avoiding waste is always important. Buying the proper amount for a canning recipe will help you stretch your dollars, as will having a canning recipe at the ready to take advantage of a sale at the grocery store.

Note: While most grocery stores are very good about reducing the price of meat well before a "best by" date, use caution when shopping sales. Even though the meat will be brought to a high temperature when pressure canning, there is no magical "undo" button for meat that is past its prime. Don't take the risk if you find meat with a bad date or that shows other signs it is past its prime. If you wouldn't grill it, don't can it.

Those new to canning may wonder why you should bother canning meat at all. Inferior canned meats, including heavily processed meat and fish, have given canned products a bad name. However, we need only look at gourmet foods and the foods of other countries to realize it doesn't have to be this way. Take, for example, some of the newer "canned" tunas on the market that come in pouches instead of cans. These packages often contain better quality tuna that has received better treatment during processing. Canned tuna can be delicious without drowning it in mayonnaise for tuna salad! Another example is the canned meat and fish in European countries, such as Spain and Portugal. It is not uncommon in a tapas bar to have something locally canned.

When canning meat at home, you're sure to change minds as well. Canning meat locks in all the flavor. While it doesn't necessarily look appetizing or sound appetizing (a jar of juicy cherries will always conjure up a nicer mental image than a jar of juicy meat), the reality is that canned meat enhances recipes. And don't forget about canned recipes that contain meat, too. That's right, in this chapter we'll also make soups and stocks.

While these recipes will guide you in a similar manner as those in the other chapters in this book, this seems like a good place to run through a few general rules and best practices for canning meat and fish.

THE BASICS

When canning meat, your first task is to find the freshest meat. If you're used to shopping at the grocery store, you may need to talk to a local butcher about the signs of how to spot fresh meat from meat that's a few days old. Common signs of fresh meat include flesh that is firm but not too dry—it bounces back quickly when pressed with a finger. Meat should also not have any strong odors. That goes for fish as well—fishy smelling fish should never be canned. You will also need to confirm the meat hasn't been previously frozen. Frozen meat or fish will have an inferior texture when canned, even if thawed before canning.

Time will be your enemy from start to finish when canning meat. You want to move your meat through the canning cycle as soon as possible and that means getting it from butcher to jars quickly. Bacteria grow fast on meats and moving efficiently through the process is the only way to be safe. Only prepare enough meat for one canner's worth of jars at a time. Do not keep meat sitting at room temperature for too long at any time—including while you make the recipe.

If you do find you have too much meat to can all at once, keep it refrigerated at 32°F to 38°F. Can it no later than the next day or use it for another recipe that doesn't require canning.

There are numerous ways to cut the meat, but, before you decide on that, you'll need to trim the meat well. Remove any bruising, fat, and silverskin you see. Fat can keep your jars from sealing well, and it can also develop a strong flavor with some types of meats. Fatty meats can also spoil more easily than lean meats. Don't worry about removing every speck, but do a thorough job trimming and you will appreciate the result.

Before you cut the meat, review your recipe. It will probably have a suggestion for how to process the meat; deviating greatly from that could make the recommended canning time unsafe. The other consideration is the meat itself. You may want to cut it with or against the grain.

The most common ways to cut meat for canning are into cubes or strips, or grinding it. With cubed meat, the goal is to create those perfect bite-size pieces. Whether the meat will go in a soup recipe or be canned on its own, cutting the pieces as uniform as possible is key. Just like with vegetables or fruit, if you have pieces that are much smaller than the rest, they will overcook—and the big danger is letting a few large cubes slip through. If they don't hit the proper temperature at the center during canning, they can harbor harmful bacteria.

Cutting meat into strips is a common treatment for steaks or roasts. If you're cooking a recipe that calls for strips, I recommend cutting *against the grain* of the meat so the strips will fit in the jar lengthwise. Cutting against the grain will result in more tender pieces. Just as with cubed meat, cutting uniformly thick strips is key. Do not can any strips that are much thicker than what the recipe specifies.

Ground meat probably looks the least appetizing once canned, yet it's also the most useful type of meat in my pantry. Ground meat is family friendly and used in many comforting recipes, from red sauce to stroganoff. Having canned ground meat on hand also makes for an easy addition to casseroles and soups. Ground meat doesn't have to be beef either. Your butcher will happily grind fresh pork, chicken, or turkey. I recommend seasoning ground meat lightly before canning. As you may use it in any number of recipes once you open the jar, if you have perfectly seasoned beef you may end up oversalting a sauce or stew.

You'll notice many recipes call for browning meat before canning. This step is key, as it's what makes your canned meat taste so much better than the "cooked in the can" variety. The browned layer goes through what is called the *Maillard reaction*, a complex interaction of sugars and amino acids that is only possible under high heat. Since you'll be fully cooking the meat when canning, the goal is usually just to create that browned layer, not cook the meat all the way through.

To make things easier when packing and unpacking jars, use wide-mouth jars when canning meat. Always leave the proper headspace as stated in the recipe, and do not fill the jars too tightly. Also, while it might be tempting to thicken the canning liquid, resist the urge. You can always thicken it after you open the jars—it's a quick process to turn the thin canned sauce into a rich, thick gravy.

THINGS TO AVOID

Following are a few things to avoid when canning meat:

* **A water bath canner.** Canning meat and fish *must be done in a pressure canner*. All meats and seafood are low-acid foods and unsafe to can using a hot water bath canner. You may have heard otherwise, but doing so is highly dangerous. It not only ruins expensive food, but can make you or your loved ones incredibly sick.

* **Thick sauces or gravies.** When canning meats, you cannot include a very thick gravy in the jar. Your meat will release its own juices and you can certainly thicken that juice when reheated, so *any gravy added to canned meats should be thin*. A good rule of thumb is to make any gravy-type liquid no thicker than tomato sauce in the jar. This allows good penetration of heat throughout the jar and into the center of each piece of meat.

* **Anything experimental.** When you can meat, it is important to follow proven recipes from reliable sources. It is no time to try new recipes or tweak the one you have. If needed, adjust the seasoning when it comes out of the jar.

CUBED PORK

We have a standing order with our butcher that I pick up each fall. He knows to call me the minute the meat is ready, as I want to get it home quickly to freeze or can. With pork, you have a good amount of leeway in the cuts you choose. As long as the meat is lean, you can cube it and can it according to the following recipe. I tend to can a variety of cuts in different base liquids to use throughout the year. Can pork in tomato juice for the beginning of a stew, in broth, or simply in salted water. The plainer the pork going in, the more versatile it is coming out—but you may find you like it best with the added flavor of broth. Whatever you choose, don't skip the browning! The flavor the pork picks up while browning can't be replicated by searing it after you can it.

**PROCESSING TIME: 1 HOUR, 15 MINUTES | PRESSURE: 10 POUNDS WEIGHTED GAUGE, 11 POUNDS DIAL GAUGE
YIELD: 4 PINTS**

3 pounds lean pork, trimmed of fat and cubed

1 quart water, tomato juice, or broth

1 teaspoon canning salt or 4 cubes of bouillon (optional)

1. Prepare 4 wide-mouth pint jars and the canner: Clean the jars and prepare the 2-piece lids according to the manufacturer's guidelines. Keep the jars in hot but not boiling water until you're ready to use them. Prepare the canner by filling it with 2 to 3 inches of water and bringing it to a simmer, or according to your manufacturer's directions.

2. In a large skillet over medium-high heat, lightly brown the pork, stirring, until it's between halfway and fully cooked. Remove the pork from the pan and set aside.

3. In a medium-size saucepan over medium-high heat, heat your liquid of choice until it reaches a boil.

4. Divide the pork evenly among the hot jars. Pour the hot liquid over the top, leaving 1 inch of headspace. If you'd like, add ¼ teaspoon salt or a bouillon cube to each jar.

5. Remove any air bubbles with a plastic or wooden utensil, adding more hot liquid as needed to maintain the proper 1-inch headspace.

6. Wipe the rims and seal the jars hand-tight with the 2-piece lids.

7. Carefully transfer the filled jars to the rack inside the pressure canner. Process the jars at the pressure listed above for 1 hour, 15 minutes.

(continued)

8. Let the canner return to 0 pounds pressure. Wait 10 minutes more, then carefully open the canner lid according to the manufacturer's instructions.

9. With a jar lifter, remove the jars and place them on a clean dishtowel away from any drafts. Once the jars cool to room temperature, check the seals. If any jars have not sealed, refrigerate them and use the pork within 1 week. Label the remaining jars with the recipe name and date before storing.

BACON JAM

How do you improve on jam? The same way you improve on almost any recipe—add bacon! Joking aside, this recipe packs big flavor with its salty-sweet goodness. Garlic, onion, and bacon meet brown sugar and maple—with a hit of tang from cider vinegar. Serve it on fancy crostini or bring it to the breakfast table. It adds punch to a bagel and cream cheese and even goes well with scrambled eggs. One other thing: This recipe is packed in tiny half-pint jars for a reason. It requires a large quantity of good-quality bacon and the last thing you want is to crack open a jar only to have it languish and expire in the fridge. On the upside, the tiny jars make great gifts. Finally, don't be in a rush when making this recipe. It requires time and care to keep the bacon from burning—trust me when I say it's worth every minute.

PROCESSING TIME: 1 HOUR, 15 MINUTES | PRESSURE: 10 POUNDS WEIGHTED GAUGE, 11 POUNDS DIAL GAUGE YIELD: 12 HALF PINTS

5 pounds good-quality bacon, cut into 1-inch pieces

5 large yellow onions, sliced into ¼-inch-thick slices

10 garlic cloves, minced

1½ cups very strong coffee

1 cup apple cider vinegar

1 cup packed brown sugar

½ cup pure maple syrup

Pepper to taste

1. In a large skillet over medium heat cook the bacon, in batches so you don't crowd the pan, until it starts to crisp, being careful not to burn it. Drain the excess fat (you may need to do this more than once), reserving 2 tablespoons. Set the bacon aside.

2. In a large pot over medium heat, combine the reserved bacon fat, onions, and garlic. Cook, stirring frequently, until the onions are translucent and the garlic is soft.

3. Stir in the coffee, vinegar, brown sugar, maple syrup, and pepper and bring the mixture to a simmer.

4. Add the cooked bacon to the onion mixture. Reduce the heat until the mixture is at a low simmer and cook for 1 hour, stirring often. If the bacon is not tender after 1 hour, continue to cook for a few minutes longer until the bacon is tender.

5. While the bacon cooks, prepare 12 wide-mouth half-pint jars and the canner: Clean the jars and prepare the 2-piece lids according to the manufacturer's guidelines. Keep the jars in hot but not boiling water until you're ready to use them. Prepare the canner by filling it with 2 to 3 inches of water and bringing it to a simmer, or according to your manufacturer's directions.

(continued)

6. Remove the bacon-onion mixture from the heat and let sit for 15 minutes to cool slightly.

7. Once the mixture cools slightly, use an immersion blender (or transfer the jam to a food processor and pulse) to break up the mixture just a bit. You want small pieces of bacon and onion, but not a smooth purée.

8. Carefully ladle the hot bacon-onion mixture into the hot jars, leaving 1 inch of headspace.

9. Remove any air bubbles with a plastic or wooden utensil, adding more hot jam as needed to maintain the proper 1-inch headspace.

10. Wipe the rims and seal the jars hand-tight with the 2-piece lids.

11. Carefully transfer the filled jars to the rack inside the pressure canner. Process the jars at the pressure listed above for 1 hour, 15 minutes.

12. Let the canner return to 0 pounds pressure. Wait 10 minutes more, then carefully open the canner lid according to the manufacturer's instructions.

13. With a jar lifter, remove the jars and place them on a clean dishtowel away from any drafts. Once the jars cool to room temperature, check the seals. If any jars have not sealed, refrigerate them and use the bacon jam within 1 week. Label the remaining jars with the recipe name and date before storing.

GROUND MEAT

Folks, this is it: the most useful (and some say the tastiest) protein in my pantry. It's always a family-wide disappointment when we run out of ground meat as I use homemade beef, pork, chicken, and turkey in a wide variety of recipes. You'll see every bit of flavor is kept in the jars during the canning process. With all that flavor, there's no need to oversalt the meat, or your dish. In fact, adding too much salt is a classic mistake—salty meat added to a perfectly seasoned soup or sauce can ruin it. As with all meats, I recommend adjusting the seasonings only after cooking and canning safely.

**PROCESSING TIME: 1 HOUR, 15 MINUTES | PRESSURE: 10 POUNDS WEIGHTED GAUGE, 11 POUNDS DIAL GAUGE
YIELD: 4 PINTS**

4 pounds ground meat of choice

1 quart water, tomato juice, or broth

1 teaspoon canning salt or 4 cubes of bouillon (optional)

1. Prepare 4 wide-mouth pint jars and the canner: Clean the jars and prepare the 2-piece lids according to the manufacturer's guidelines. Keep the jars in hot but not boiling water until you're ready to use them. Prepare the canner by filling it with 2 to 3 inches of water and bringing it to a simmer, or according to your manufacturer's directions.

2. In a large skillet over medium-high heat, and working in batches if necessary, fry the meat until it is lightly browned and about halfway cooked. Don't overload your pan trying to cook all the meat at once—the browning is crucial to this recipe.

3. In a medium-size saucepan over medium-high heat, heat your liquid of choice until it reaches a boil.

4. Divide the ground meat among the jars, packing it loosely. Pour the hot liquid into the hot jars over the meat, leaving 1 inch of headspace. If you'd like, add ¼ teaspoon salt or a bouillon cube to each jar.

5. Remove any air bubbles with a plastic or wooden utensil, adding more hot liquid as needed to maintain the proper 1-inch headspace.

6. Wipe the rims and seal the jars hand-tight with the 2-piece lids.

7. Carefully transfer the filled jars to the rack inside the pressure canner. Process the jars at the pressure listed above for 1 hour, 15 minutes.

8. Let the canner return to 0 pounds pressure. Wait 10 minutes more, then carefully open the canner lid according to the manufacturer's instructions.

9. With a jar lifter, remove the jars and place them on a clean dishtowel away from any drafts. Once the jars cool to room temperature, check the seals. If any jars have not sealed, refrigerate them and use the meat within 1 week. Label the remaining jars with the recipe name and date before storing.

CANNED CHICKEN

Commercially made canned chicken must be one of the more dreadful canned meats. Chicken doesn't have the strong flavor of foods like tuna to cover the flavor imparted by the can. As if the producers wanted to make it worse, the quality of meat used for canned chicken is often not as high as chicken sold fresh. It may well be a blend of cuts, labeled as "with rib meat," or similar. Obviously, homemade canned chicken doesn't suffer from the same problems. You choose the cuts and quality and you process it in jars instead of cans. This chicken is ready straight from the can, and not just for chicken salad. Try it in any recipe where you'd use a store-bought rotisserie chicken. My family is partial to wrapping it as chicken verde burritos.

**PROCESSING TIME: 1 HOUR, 15 MINUTES | PRESSURE: 10 POUNDS WEIGHTED GAUGE, 11 POUNDS DIAL GAUGE
YIELD: 4 PINTS**

4 pounds boneless, skinless chicken, trimmed of fat and cut into 1-inch cubes

1 teaspoon canning salt (optional)

1. Prepare 4 wide-mouth pint jars and the canner: Clean the jars and prepare the 2-piece lids according to the manufacturer's guidelines. Keep the jars in hot but not boiling water until you're ready to use them. Prepare the canner by filling it with 2 to 3 inches of water and bringing it to a simmer, or according to your manufacturer's directions.

2. Fill the jars loosely with the raw chicken, leaving 1¼ inches of headspace (see Note). Add ¼ tsp salt to each jar, if desired.

3. Wipe the rims and seal the jars hand-tight with the 2-piece lids.

4. Carefully transfer the filled jars to the rack inside the pressure canner. Process the jars at the pressure listed above for 1 hour, 15 minutes.

5. Let the canner return to 0 pounds pressure. Wait 10 minutes more, then carefully open the canner lid according to the manufacturer's instructions.

6. With a jar lifter, remove the jars and place them on a clean dishtowel away from any drafts. Once the jars cool to room temperature, check the seals. If any jars have not sealed, refrigerate them and use the chicken within 1 week. Label the remaining jars with the recipe name and date before storing.

NOTE

Yes, the headspace for this recipe is more than 1 inch, so there's a bit of extra room in the jars. The chicken will release its natural juices during cooking, so you will not need to add water before canning.

CANNED HADDOCK

Living on the coast, canning seafood and fish just makes sense. It's a "local" food, after all. Although I freeze much of it, having it ready to eat on the shelf provides another option. It's become a yearly tradition for my family to order haddock from a local fisherman and can it right after the catch. I use this mild-flavored fish like I would tuna: for fish burgers, in fish soup, and as the star of savory chowders. By keeping the flavoring plain when canning, it's easy to spice it up however I need to for a meal. I can dozens of jars, but there is no need to save so much of it if your family doesn't eat as much fish. If you can buy fresh fish in any quantity, try to save some for your shelf. It's wonderful!

PROCESSING TIME: 1 HOUR, 40 MINUTES | PRESSURE: 10 POUNDS WEIGHTED GAUGE, 11 POUNDS DIAL GAUGE | YIELD: 6 PINTS

---

12 pounds haddock, or similar freshwater fish fillets

6 teaspoons canning salt

1. Prepare 6 wide-mouth pint jars and the canner: Clean the jars and prepare the 2-piece lids according to the manufacturer's guidelines. Keep the jars in hot but not boiling water until you're ready to use them. Prepare the canner by filling it with 2 to 3 inches of water and bringing it to a simmer, or according to your manufacturer's directions.

2. Make sure your fillets don't have any stray entrails, scales, or pieces of the head, tail, or fins. Cut the fish into pieces short enough to fit in the jars, keeping in mind the 1-inch required headspace. Cut the pieces as close as possible to uniform thickness. Fill the jars with the fish, placing the pieces around the outside of the jar for a neater look, and filling the center with the less than perfect pieces, leaving 1 inch of headspace.

3. Add 1 teaspoon of salt to each jar. Like canned chicken, you do not need to add any water to fill the jars.

4. Wipe the rims and seal the jars hand-tight with the 2-piece lids.

5. Carefully transfer the filled jars to the rack inside the pressure canner. Process the jars at the pressure listed above for 1 hour, 40 minutes.

6. Let the canner return to 0 pounds pressure. Wait 10 minutes more, then carefully open the canner lid according to the manufacturer's instructions.

7. With a jar lifter, remove the jars and place them on a clean dishtowel away from any drafts. Once the jars cool to room temperature, check the seals. If any jars have not sealed, refrigerate them and use the fish within 1 week. Label the remaining jars with the recipe name and date before storing.

BE PREPARED WHEN CANNING FISH

Canning fish is not something I recommend for the beginning canner. It's best to start canning easier items, like vegetables and fruits, move on to meat and soups, and finally try your hand at fish.

Being a delicate meat, fish needs to be prepared as quickly and carefully as possible. Don't wait until the day you are going to buy or catch your fish for canning; be sure you have all your supplies beforehand.

Here on the coast we contact our local haddock fisherman and make plans to pick up 50 pounds of haddock on a specific time and date. I prepare my canning equipment and check that I have enough lids. (Because for some reason I never do!) When my husband brings home a heavy box of haddock fillets, I am ready to get to work.

THANKSGIVING TURKEY SOUP

This soup tastes like Thanksgiving in a jar. I often use the turkey bones from the big day to make the broth and throw in a little of the leftover turkey from our meal. Since I brine my turkey the night before, the meat starts out moist. I experimented by adding the cranberries one year and now I do it every time. Try it and you'll see—they seem to pull the whole recipe together.

PROCESSING TIME: 1 HOUR | PRESSURE: 10 POUNDS WEIGHTED GAUGE, 11 POUNDS DIAL GAUGE
YIELD: 4 PINTS

2 quarts Chicken or
Turkey Broth (page 177),
or store-bought broth

½ cup sliced celery

½ cup sliced carrot

½ large yellow onion,
chopped

1 cup fresh or canned
and drained corn

½ cup chopped fresh
cranberries

1 cup shredded cooked
turkey

1 cup Great Northern
beans, cooked and
drained

1 fresh sage leaf, or ½
teaspoon dried sage

Salt and pepper to taste

1. Prepare 4 wide-mouth pint jars and the canner: Clean the jars and prepare the 2-piece lids according to the manufacturer's guidelines. Keep the jars in hot but not boiling water until you're ready to use them. Prepare the canner by filling it with 2 to 3 inches of water and bringing it to a simmer, or according to your manufacturer's directions.

2. In a large stockpot over medium-high heat, combine the broth, celery, carrot, onion, corn, and cranberries. Cover the pot and bring to a simmer.

3. Add the turkey, beans, and sage. Season with salt and pepper. Continue cooking until the soup comes to a boil.

4. Carefully ladle the hot soup into the hot jars, leaving 1 inch of headspace.

5. Remove any air bubbles with a plastic or wooden utensil, adding more hot soup as needed to maintain the proper 1-inch headspace.

6. Wipe the rims and seal the jars hand-tight with the 2-piece lids.

7. Carefully transfer the filled jars to the rack inside the pressure canner. Process the jars at the pressure listed above for 1 hour.

8. Let the canner return to 0 pounds pressure. Wait 10 minutes more, then carefully open the canner lid according to the manufacturer's instructions.

9. With a jar lifter, remove the jars and place them on a clean dishtowel away from any drafts. Once the jars cool to room temperature, check the seals. If any jars have not sealed, refrigerate them and use the soup within 1 week. Label the remaining jars with the recipe name and date before storing.

PRESSURE CANNING SOUPS

There is nothing like a comforting bowl of soup after a long day at work, as the perfect lunch, or when you don't feel well. Like most foods, home-canned soups taste better than store-bought cans—and you can leave out the questionable preservatives.

Making soups for canning is almost the same as making them to serve immediately for dinner. There are just a few simple rules to follow to be sure your soups are canned safely.

1. Do not add starches such as noodles and rice to your canned soups. These foods become mushy and fall apart during the canning process. Even if the soups look good after the jars come out of the canner, reheating the soup will result in a breakdown of the starches and an undesirable mushy texture. Add the rice or noodles to the soup after you crack the jar to serve it.

2. When canning soups, add more broth than you would when making it on the stovetop. I fill my jars one-fourth of the way with vegetables and meat and the rest of the way with broth.

3. Cooled soup may thicken slightly in the jar when using homemade meat broths. If this happens, it's completely normal. Once you reheat the soup, it will quickly thin again.

4. Some ingredients do not belong in canned soups as they become so strong in flavor they overwhelm the recipe—broccoli, cabbage, and brussels sprouts all taste too intense after canning, in my opinion. If you want to experiment with these ingredients, use less than you normally would so they don't overpower your recipe.

5. When adding dried beans to your soups, cook them before adding to the recipe. Dry beans absorb quite a bit of moisture and will absorb too much broth.

MEXICAN CHICKEN SOUP

Slightly spicy, this soup is just right with a piece of fresh cornbread. I love serving it with a dollop of sour cream as well. Make it as spicy as you like. My family falls into the "medium heat" category, but the base recipe here is as mild as the taco seasoning you use. To spice it up, leave in some or all of the jalapeño seeds and add a few dashes of hot sauce when serving.

PROCESSING TIME: 1 HOUR | **PRESSURE: 10 POUNDS WEIGHTED GAUGE, 11 POUNDS DIAL GAUGE**
YIELD: 4 PINTS

2 quarts Chicken or Turkey Broth (page 177), or store-bought broth

½ cup sliced celery

½ large yellow onion, chopped

2 garlic cloves, sliced

1 cup diced tomatoes

1 cup fresh or canned and drained corn

1 jalapeño pepper, seeded and minced

1 cup shredded cooked chicken

1 cup canned and drained black beans

2 teaspoons taco seasoning

Salt to taste

1. Prepare 4 wide-mouth pint jars and the canner: Clean the jars and prepare the 2-piece lids according to the manufacturer's guidelines. Keep the jars in hot but not boiling water until you're ready to use them. Prepare the canner by filling it with 2 to 3 inches of water and bringing it to a simmer, or according to your manufacturer's directions.

2. In a large stockpot over medium-high heat, combine the broth, celery, onion, garlic, tomatoes, corn, and jalapeño. Cover the pot and bring to a simmer.

3. Stir in the chicken, black beans, and taco seasoning. Taste and add salt, if desired. Continue to heat the broth to a boil.

4. Carefully ladle the hot soup into the hot jars, leaving 1 inch of headspace.

5. Remove any air bubbles with a plastic or wooden utensil, adding more hot soup as needed to maintain the proper 1-inch headspace.

6. Wipe the rims and seal the jars hand-tight with the 2-piece lids.

7. Carefully transfer the filled jars to the rack inside the pressure canner. Process the jars at the pressure listed above for 1 hour.

8. Let the canner return to 0 pounds pressure. Wait 10 minutes more, then carefully open the canner lid according to the manufacturer's instructions.

9. With a jar lifter, remove the jars and place them on a clean dishtowel away from any drafts. Once the jars cool to room temperature, check the seals. If any jars have not sealed, refrigerate them and use the soup within 1 week. Label the remaining jars with the recipe name and date before storing.

CHICKEN SOUP

I first started canning my own soup when I realized how much better the homemade versions of my childhood soups tasted. It's also a convenient meal: a pint of chicken soup and a couple of grilled sandwiches make for a filling meal in minutes. It saves me time and money for months if I can a few dozen jars for the winter. You may substitute your favorite vegetables in this recipe, but do *not* add any starch, such as rice or noodles. Starches break down during the canning process.

PROCESSING TIME: 1 HOUR | **PRESSURE: 10 POUNDS WEIGHTED GAUGE, 11 POUNDS DIAL GAUGE**
YIELD: 6 PINTS

1½ quarts Chicken or Turkey Broth (page 177), or store-bought broth

2 cups canned and drained corn kernels

1 cup chopped onion

1 cup sliced carrot

1 cup sliced celery

1 cup fresh or frozen peas

1 cup canned and drained chickpeas

1 whole bay leaf,

2 fresh sage leaves, crumbled

Salt and pepper to taste

2 cups chopped cooked chicken

1. Prepare 6 wide-mouth pint jars and the canner: Clean the jars and prepare the 2-piece lids according to the manufacturer's guidelines. Keep the jars in hot but not boiling water until you're ready to use them. Prepare the canner by filling it with 2 to 3 inches of water and bringing it to a simmer, or according to your manufacturer's directions.

2. In a large stockpot over medium-high heat, combine the broth, corn, onion, carrot, celery, peas, chickpeas, bay leaf, and sage. Season with salt and pepper. Bring the soup to a simmer. Taste and adjust the seasonings, as you like.

3. Using a funnel to keep the rims clean, divide the chicken evenly among the jars, filling them about one-fourth full.

4. Carefully pour the hot soup over the chicken and fill the jars, leaving 1 inch of headspace.

5. Remove any air bubbles with a plastic or wooden utensil, adding liquid as needed to maintain the proper 1-inch headspace.

6. Wipe the rims and seal the jars hand-tight with the 2-piece lids.

7. Carefully transfer the filled jars to the rack inside the pressure canner. Process the jars at the pressure listed above for 1 hour.

8. Let the canner return to 0 pounds pressure. Wait 10 minutes more, then carefully open the canner lid according to the manufacturer's instructions.

9. With a jar lifter, remove the jars and place them on a clean dishtowel away from any drafts. Once the jars cool to room temperature, check the seals. If any jars have not sealed, refrigerate them and use the soup within 1 week. Label the remaining jars with the recipe name and date before storing.

BEEF SOUP WITH LENTILS

Beef soup with lentils is a go-to dish when I want to get my kids to eat some beans. This is the heartiest soup I make, which makes it perfect after a long day of sledding or climbing around the beach during low tide in winter. It's filling on its own but I recommend serving it with a thick slice of homemade bread on the side.

PROCESSING TIME: 1 HOUR | **PRESSURE: 10 POUNDS WEIGHTED GAUGE, 11 POUNDS DIAL GAUGE**
YIELD: 4 PINTS

2 quarts broth of your choice

1 cup peeled and cubed potato

½ cup sliced celery

½ large yellow onion, chopped

½ cup sliced carrot

½ cup fresh or canned and drained corn

1 cup shredded cooked beef

1 cup lentils, cooked and drained

1 bay leaf

Salt and pepper to taste

1. Prepare 4 wide-mouth pint jars and the canner: Clean the jars and prepare the 2-piece lids according to the manufacturer's guidelines. Keep the jars in hot but not boiling water until you're ready to use them. Prepare the canner by filling it with 2 to 3 inches of water and bringing it to a simmer, or according to your manufacturer's directions.

2. In a large stockpot over medium-high heat, combine the broth, potato, celery, onion, carrot, and corn. Cover the pot and bring to a simmer.

3. Add the beef, lentils, and bay leaf. Season with salt and pepper. Continue cooking until the soup comes to a boil.

4. Carefully ladle the hot soup into the hot jars, leaving 1 inch of headspace.

5. Remove any air bubbles with a plastic or wooden utensil, adding more hot soup as needed to maintain the proper 1-inch headspace.

6. Wipe the rims and seal the jars hand-tight with the 2-piece lids.

7. Carefully transfer the filled jars to the rack inside the pressure canner. Process the jars at the pressure listed above for 1 hour.

8. Let the canner return to 0 pounds pressure. Wait 10 minutes more, then carefully open the canner lid according to the manufacturer's instructions.

9. With a jar lifter, remove the jars and place them on a clean dishtowel away from any drafts. Once the jars cool to room temperature, check the seals. If any jars have not sealed, refrigerate them and use the soup within 1 week. Label the remaining jars with the recipe name and date before storing.

MEATBALLS IN TOMATO JUICE

Nobody will turn down homemade meat sauce. Yet I think 9 out of 10 people prefer red sauce with meatballs. While I normally serve these simply, with buttered noodles, it also works as the base of a tomato and vegetable soup. Since you'll be forming meatballs instead of canning ground meat, you will need to pay careful attention both to how you pack the meatballs and how consistent in size they are. Use a large spoon or small ice cream scoop that gives you perfect 1-inch meatballs. That way, if you get a bit distracted toward the end, you will still maintain that all-important consistency.

PROCESSING TIME: 1 HOUR, 15 MINUTES | PRESSURE: 10 POUNDS WEIGHTED GAUGE, 11 POUNDS DIAL GAUGE YIELD: 4 PINTS

3 pounds ground beef

½ cup minced onion

3 cups soft (fresh) bread crumbs

3 eggs

Salt and pepper to taste

1 quart tomato juice

1. Preheat the oven to 450°F.

2. Meanwhile, prepare 4 wide-mouth pint jars and the canner: Clean the jars and prepare the 2-piece lids according to the manufacturer's guidelines. Keep the jars in hot but not boiling water until you're ready to use them. Prepare the canner by filling it with 2 to 3 inches of water and bringing it to a simmer, or according to your manufacturer's directions.

3. In a large bowl, combine the ground meat, onion, bread crumbs, and eggs. Season with salt and pepper. Mix by hand until well combined. Using a small ice cream scoop, or by hand, form the meat mixture into 1-inch meatballs and place them on a jelly-roll pan or rimmed baking sheet. Bake for 15 minutes. Remove from the oven and set aside.

4. In a medium-size saucepan over medium heat, heat the tomato juice until it boils.

5. Pack the meatballs into the hot jars. Carefully pour the hot juice over the meatballs and fill the jars, leaving 1 inch of headspace.

6. Remove any air bubbles with a plastic or wooden utensil, adding more hot juice as needed to maintain the proper 1-inch headspace.

7. Wipe the rims and seal the jars hand-tight with the 2-piece lids.

8. Carefully transfer the filled jars to the rack inside the pressure canner. Process the jars at the pressure listed above for 1 hour, 15 minutes.

9. Let the canner return to 0 pounds pressure. Wait 10 minutes more, then carefully open the canner lid according to the manufacturer's instructions.

10. With a jar lifter, remove the jars and place them on a clean dishtowel away from any drafts. Once the jars cool to room temperature, check the seals. If any jars have not sealed, refrigerate them and use the meatballs within 1 week. Label the remaining jars with the recipe name and date before storing.

CHAPTER SEVEN

SALSA, SAUCE, AND BROTH RECIPES

NO MATTER HOW MANY OF THE RECIPES in this chapter I can and save, by the end of the winter they're always gone. The recipe for classic Tomato Sauce (page 163) is a great example. As is, it has just enough seasoning to go a number of ways when you're ready to eat it. You can add seasoned meat to it or a mix of fresh stir-fried vegetables.

Canning salsa is a much-anticipated activity on our farm. I make a big deal out of how hot it might end up tasting each year, as we grow many types of hot peppers. My recipe is super simple, too. It showcases the fresh peppers, onions, and ripe tomatoes.

Wait, didn't I say these recipes make meals in the winter? How does salsa get a meal going? Well, in addition to spicing up taco night, it makes a flavorful addition to soups, can be the start of a simmer sauce for meats, and it's the perfect condiment for healthy veggie bowls.

TOMATO SAUCE

This basic sauce is the beginning of a long list of meals around here. We tend to have pasta once a week, and I also use this red sauce to start many a chili, soup, and casserole. A well-seasoned sauce is one of the most useful foods on the pantry shelf.

**PROCESSING TIME: 25 MINUTES | PRESSURE: 10 POUNDS WEIGHTED GAUGE, 11 POUNDS DIAL GAUGE
YIELD: 5 PINTS**

2 medium-size onions, chopped

2 garlic cloves, minced

2 carrots, shredded

2 celery stalks, finely chopped

8 ounces mushrooms, sliced

2 quarts stewed tomatoes (canned is fine), including the liquid

2 (6-ounce) cans tomato paste

1 cup dry red wine

1 cup chopped fresh parsley leaves

1 tablespoon chopped fresh basil leaves

1 teaspoon salt (optional)

Freshly ground pepper

1. In a large, heavy-bottomed pot over medium heat, combine the onions, garlic, carrots, celery, and mushrooms. Cook, stirring frequently, until the vegetables start to sweat and soften.

2. Stir in the tomatoes, tomato paste, wine, parsley, basil, and salt (if using). Season with pepper. Stir again to combine. Cook the sauce until it comes to a boil, stirring frequently. Once the sauce reaches a boil, immediately reduce the heat to low and simmer for 2 hours, uncovered, stirring often.

3. Meanwhile, prepare 5 pint jars and the canner: Clean the jars and prepare the 2-piece lids according to the manufacturer's guidelines. Keep the jars in hot but not boiling water until you're ready to use them. Prepare the canner by filling it with 2 to 3 inches of water and bringing it to a simmer, or according to your manufacturer's directions.

4. Carefully ladle hot sauce into the hot jars, leaving 1 inch of headspace.

5. Remove any air bubbles with a plastic or wooden utensil, adding more hot sauce as needed to maintain the proper 1-inch headspace.

6. Wipe the rims and seal the jars hand-tight with the 2-piece lids.

7. Carefully transfer the filled jars to the rack inside the pressure canner. Process the jars at the pressure listed above for 25 minutes.

8. Let the canner return to 0 pounds pressure. Wait 10 minutes more, then carefully open the canner lid according to the manufacturer's instructions.

9. With a jar lifter, remove the jars and place them on a clean dishtowel away from any drafts. Once the jars cool to room temperature, check the seals. If any jars have not sealed, refrigerate them and use the sauce within 2 weeks. Label the remaining jars with the recipe name and date before storing.

TACO SAUCE

Our version of Mexican night is pretty tame by most standards, but we love the slightly spicy taste of this recipe. Use it with the ground meat of your choice or get creative: I've found I can get as many vegetables as I want into my kids when I flavor them with this sauce. That said, it's not authentic. If you are a purist, be forewarned!

PROCESSING TIME: 15 MINUTES | **PRESSURE: 10 POUNDS WEIGHTED GAUGE, 11 POUNDS DIAL GAUGE**
YIELD: 4 PINTS

8 cups peeled, chopped, and drained tomatoes,

1 medium-size onion, chopped

1 cup chopped scallion

½ cup chopped seeded jalapeño peppers, or other green chile

4 garlic cloves, chopped

1 teaspoon salt

1 teaspoon chili powder

½ teaspoon ground cumin

1. Prepare 4 pint jars and the canner: Clean the jars and prepare the 2-piece lids according to the manufacturer's guidelines. Keep the jars in hot but not boiling water until you're ready to use them. Prepare the canner by filling it with 2 to 3 inches of water and bringing it to a simmer, or according to your manufacturer's directions.

2. In a saucepan over medium heat, combine the tomatoes, onion, scallion, jalapeños, garlic, salt, chili powder, and cumin. Stir to combine and bring to a simmer. Simmer for 30 minutes, stirring frequently.

3. Strain the sauce through a fine-mesh strainer and return it to the pan. Bring the sauce to a boil and cook for 5 minutes.

4. Carefully ladle the hot sauce into the hot jars, leaving 1 inch of headspace.

5. Remove any air bubbles with a plastic or wooden utensil, adding more hot sauce as needed to maintain the proper 1-inch headspace.

6. Wipe the rims and seal the jars hand-tight with the 2-piece lids.

7. Carefully transfer the filled jars to the rack inside the pressure canner. Process the jars at the pressure listed above for 15 minutes.

8. Let the canner return to 0 pounds pressure. Wait 10 minutes more, then carefully open the canner lid according to the manufacturer's instructions.

9. With a jar lifter, remove the jars and place them on a clean dishtowel away from any drafts. One the jars cool to room temperature, check the seals. If any jars have not sealed, refrigerate them and use the sauce within 2 weeks.

TOMATO SALSA

Bright with the flavor of perfectly ripe summer tomatoes, this is the most versatile salsa I have ever made. I use it for everything from chips and salsa to seasoning my pot roast in the slow cooker. Make it as hot or mild as you like. I try to put up some with different spice levels to satisfy everyone.

PROCESSING TIME: 10 MINUTES | PRESSURE: 10 POUNDS WEIGHTED GAUGE, 11 POUNDS DIAL GAUGE
YIELD: 4 PINTS

10 ripe paste-type tomatoes, such as Roma

2 onions, chopped

2 green bell peppers, seeded and chopped

2 chile peppers, seeded and chopped (or include the seeds for more heat)

1 jalapeño pepper, seeded and chopped (or include the seeds for more heat)

2 garlic cloves, minced

¼ cup freshly squeezed lemon juice (from about 2 lemons)

1 tablespoon salt (or to taste)

1 teaspoon freshly ground black pepper (or to taste)

1. Prepare 4 pint jars and the canner: Clean the jars and prepare the 2-piece lids according to the manufacturer's guidelines. Keep the jars in hot but not boiling water until you're ready to use them. Prepare the canner by filling it with 2 to 3 inches of water and bringing it to a simmer, or according to your manufacturer's directions.

2. Prepare an ice-water bath and bring a medium-size saucepan of water to a boil.

3. Remove the tomato skins: Working 1 tomato at a time for best results, place the tomato into the boiling water for 1 minute. Transfer to the ice-water bath. The skins will split and peel off easily. Chop the peeled tomatoes.

4. Empty the pan and return it to medium-high heat. In it, combine the tomatoes, onions, green bell peppers, chile and jalapeño peppers, and garlic. Stir in the lemon juice. Bring the salsa to a boil. Once the salsa is warm, taste and season with salt and pepper as needed. Reduce the heat to low and simmer the salsa for 15 minutes, stirring frequently.

5. Carefully ladle the hot salsa into the hot jars, leaving ¾ inch of headspace.

6. Remove any air bubbles with a plastic or wooden utensil, adding more hot salsa as needed to maintain the proper ¾-inch headspace.

7. Wipe the rims and seal the jars hand-tight with the 2-piece lids.

8. Carefully transfer the filled jars to the rack inside the pressure canner. Process the jars at the pressure listed above for 10 minutes.

9. Let the canner return to 0 pounds pressure. Wait 10 minutes more, then carefully open the canner lid according to the manufacturer's instructions.

10. With a jar lifter, remove the jars and place them on a clean dishtowel away from any drafts. Once the jars cool to room temperature, check the seals. If any jars have not sealed, refrigerate them and use the salsa within 2 weeks.

PEACH TOMATO SALSA

While I normally advocate only the freshest fruits and vegetables when canning, this salsa is an exception. It is a wonderful way to use peaches that aren't quite ripe. As with most fruit salsas, this is a great condiment not only for tacos, but for fish and chicken as well.

PROCESSING TIME: 10 MINUTES | PRESSURE: 10 POUNDS WEIGHTED GAUGE, 11 POUNDS DIAL GAUGE
YIELD: 6 PINTS

2 pounds paste-type tomatoes, such as Roma

3 pounds peaches, chopped

2½ cups chopped onion

2 cups chopped green bell pepper

2 cups chopped peeled apple

1 tablespoon salt

1 teaspoon red pepper flakes

3¾ cups packed light brown sugar

2¼ cups apple cider vinegar

¼ cup pickling spice, tied in a muslin bag

1. Prepare 6 pint jars and the canner: Clean the jars and prepare the 2-piece lids according to the manufacturer's guidelines. Keep the jars in hot but not boiling water until you're ready to use them. Prepare the canner by filling it with 2 to 3 inches of water and bringing it to a simmer, or according to your manufacturer's directions.

2. Prepare an ice-water bath and bring a large saucepan of water to a boil.

3. Remove the tomato skins: Working 1 tomato at a time for best results, place the tomato into the boiling water for 1 minute. Transfer to the ice-water bath. The skins will split and peel off easily. Chop the peeled tomatoes.

4. Empty the pan and return it to medium-high heat. In it, combine the tomatoes, peaches, onion, green bell pepper, apple, salt, red pepper flakes, brown sugar, vinegar, and the muslin bag containing the pickling spices.

5. As the mixture starts to warm, stir to incorporate everything. Bring the mixture to a boil, stirring frequently to keep it from burning. Once the mixture boils, reduce the heat to low, and simmer for 30 minutes.

6. Remove and discard the muslin bag and turn off the heat.

7. Carefully ladle the salsa into the hot jars, leaving ½ inch of headspace.

8. Remove any air bubbles with a plastic or wooden utensil, adding more hot salsa as needed to maintain the proper ½-inch headspace.

9. Wipe the rims and seal the jars hand-tight with the 2-piece lids.

10. Carefully transfer the filled jars to the rack inside the pressure canner. Process the jars at the pressure listed above for 10 minutes.

11. Let the canner return to 0 pounds pressure. Wait 10 minutes more, then carefully open the canner lid according to the manufacturer's instructions.

12. With a jar lifter, remove the jars and place them on a clean dishtowel away from any drafts. Once the jars cool to room temperature, check the seals. If any jars have not sealed, refrigerate them and use the salsa within 1 week.

TOMATILLO SALSA

For a change of pace, I like to make and serve this green, not-so-spicy salsa for everyday eating. If you're unfamiliar with tomatillo salsa, it is quite a departure from a classic red tomato salsa. The tomatillos have a unique flavor to start—tart, fruity, and slightly herbal. Throw in a good amount of vinegar and cilantro and you end up with a bright, fresh flavor. Use it as you would any salsa, as a dip or a topping for tacos. Or try a recipe that features the salsa, such as enchiladas verde.

PROCESSING TIME: 15 MINUTES | PRESSURE: 10 POUNDS WEIGHTED GAUGE, 11 POUNDS DIAL GAUGE
YIELD: 2 PINTS

2 pounds tomatillos, cleaned, cored, and diced into small pieces

1 large onion, roughly chopped

4 large Anaheim chiles, seeded

4 garlic cloves, peeled

1 cup distilled white vinegar

¼ cup freshly squeezed lime juice (from about 2 limes)

2 tablespoons minced fresh cilantro leaves

2 teaspoons ground cumin

½ teaspoon canning salt

½ teaspoon red pepper flakes

1. Prepare 2 pint jars and the canner: Clean the jars and prepare the 2-piece lids according to the manufacturer's guidelines. Keep the jars in hot but not boiling water until you're ready to use them. Prepare the canner by filling it with 2 to 3 inches of water and bringing it to a simmer, or according to your manufacturer's directions.

2. Place the tomatillos in a large pot.

3. In a food processor, combine the onion, chiles, and garlic. Pulse a few times until the vegetables are broken into very small pieces. Add them to the tomatillos. Bring the mixture to a boil over high heat.

4. As the mixture starts to warm, add the vinegar, lime juice, cilantro, cumin, canning salt, and red pepper flakes. Stir well to incorporate the ingredients. Once the salsa boils, reduce the heat to low, and simmer for 10 minutes.

5. Carefully ladle the hot salsa into the hot jars, leaving 1 inch of headspace.

6. Remove any air bubbles with a plastic or wooden utensil, adding more hot salsa as needed to maintain the proper 1-inch headspace.

7. Wipe the rims and seal the jars hand-tight with the 2-piece lids.

8. Carefully transfer the filled jars to the rack inside the pressure canner. Process the jars at the pressure listed above for 15 minutes.

9. Let the canner return to 0 pounds pressure. Wait 10 minutes more, then carefully open the canner lid according to the manufacturer's instructions.

10. With a jar lifter, remove the jars and place them on a clean dishtowel away from any drafts. Once the jars cool to room temperature, check the seals. If any jars have not sealed, refrigerate them and use the salsa within 2 weeks.

GREEN TOMATO CHUTNEY

No matter how early I plant my tomatoes, I always end up with plenty that don't have a hint of red on them by first frost. I used to be upset by these stragglers until I found recipes like this that put green tomatoes to good use. Now, I'm actually quite happy if there are plenty of green tomatoes remaining at the end of gardening season.

PROCESSING TIME: 10 MINUTES | **PRESSURE: 10 POUNDS WEIGHTED GAUGE, 11 POUNDS DIAL GAUGE**
YIELD: 4 PINTS

10 paste-type tomatoes, such as Roma

2 onions, chopped

2 green bell peppers, seeded and chopped

2 garlic cloves, minced

2 chile peppers, such as Thai chiles, seeded and chopped (or include the seeds for more heat)

1 jalapeño pepper, seeded and chopped (or include the seeds for more heat)

¼ cup freshly squeezed lemon juice (from about 2 lemons)

1 tablespoon salt

1 teaspoon freshly ground black pepper

2 tablespoons chopped fresh cilantro leaves

1. Prepare 4 pint jars and the canner: Clean the jars and prepare the 2-piece lids according to the manufacturer's guidelines. Keep the jars in hot but not boiling water until you're ready to use them. Prepare the canner by filling it with 2 to 3 inches of water and bringing it to a simmer, or according to your manufacturer's directions.

2. Prepare an ice-water bath and bring a large pot of water to a boil.

3. Remove the tomato skins: Working 1 tomato at a time for best results, place the tomato into the boiling water for 1 minute. Transfer to the ice-water bath. The skins will split and peel off easily. Chop the peeled tomatoes.

4. Empty the pot and return it to medium-high heat. In it, combine the tomatoes, onions, green bell pepper, garlic, chile and jalapeño peppers, lemon juice, salt, pepper, and cilantro. Stir to combine. Bring the mixture to a boil. Reduce the heat to low and simmer for 15 minutes, stirring frequently.

5. Carefully ladle the hot chutney into the hot jars, leaving ¾ inch of headspace.

6. Remove air bubbles with a plastic or wooden utensil, adding more hot chutney as needed to maintain the proper ¾-inch headspace.

7. Wipe the rims and seal the jars hand-tight with the 2-piece lids.

8. Carefully transfer the filled jars to the rack inside the pressure canner. Process the jars at the pressure listed above for 10 minutes.

9. Let the canner return to 0 pounds pressure. Wait 10 minutes more, then carefully open the canner lid according to the manufacturer's instructions.

10. With a jar lifter, remove the jars and place them on a clean dishtowel away from any drafts. Once the jars cool to room temperature, check the seals. If any jars have not sealed, refrigerate them and use the chutney within 2 weeks.

BARBECUE SAUCE

Every spring, we break out the grill long before the last snow. It must be funny to see us gathered around a smoking grill in our winter coats! With such a strong urge to grill, it's no surprise we use more barbecue sauce than the average family. I have to put up quite a bit so we don't run out.

Barbecue sauces vary by region and by personal preference, so I suppose I should tell you what our house sauce is like—it's thick but not too sweet, with just enough smoky flavor to enhance a good cut of meat. We usually wait until the food is cooked and add the sauce during the last minute or two. That way it flavors well, but the sugars in the sauce don't have a chance to burn.

PROCESSING TIME: 15 MINUTES | PRESSURE: 10 POUNDS WEIGHTED GAUGE, 11 POUNDS DIAL GAUGE YIELD: 2 PINTS

2 quarts Roma tomatoes

1 cup chopped onion

1 green bell pepper, seeded and chopped

1 hot pepper, such as jalapeño or serrano, seeded and minced

1 garlic clove, minced

½ cup packed dark brown sugar

1½ teaspoons smoked paprika

1½ teaspoons salt

½ cup plus 2 table-spoons white or apple cider vinegar, 5%

1. Prepare 2 pint jars and the canner: Clean the jars and prepare the 2-piece lids according to the manufacturer's guidelines. Keep the jars in hot but not boiling water until you're ready to use them. Prepare the canner by filling it with 2 to 3 inches of water and bringing it to a simmer, or according to your manufacturer's directions.

2. Prepare an ice-water bath and bring a large saucepan of water to a boil.

3. Remove the tomato skins: Working 1 tomato at a time for best results, place the tomato into the boiling water for 1 minute. Transfer to the ice-water bath. The skins will split and peel off easily. Chop the peeled tomatoes.

4. In a large stockpot over medium heat, combine the chopped tomatoes, onion, green bell pepper, hot pepper, garlic, brown sugar, paprika, salt, and vinegar. Cook for about 30 minutes, until the vegetables are very soft.

5. Remove the pot from the heat and use an immersion blender or food mill to purée the sauce as much as possible. Strain the sauce through a fine-mesh to remove any large pieces. At this point you should have a nice smooth sauce. Return the sauce to the heat and simmer until it has reduced by half, about 45 minutes.

6. Carefully ladle the hot barbecue sauce into the hot jars, leaving ½ inch of headspace.

7. Remove any air bubbles with a plastic or wooden utensil, adding more hot barbecue sauce as needed to maintain the proper ½-inch headspace.

8. Wipe the rims and seal the jars hand-tight with the 2-piece lids.

9. Carefully transfer the filled jars to the rack inside the pressure canner. Process the jars at the pressure listed above for 15 minutes.

10. Let the canner return to 0 pounds pressure. Wait 10 minutes more, then carefully open the canner lid according to the manufacturer's instructions.

11. With a jar lifter, remove the jars and place them on a clean dishtowel away from any drafts. Once the jars cool to room temperature, check the seals. If any jars have not sealed, refrigerate them and use the barbecue sauce within 2 weeks.

TOMATO KETCHUP

Richer in tomato flavor and much less sweet, this is a reason to make french fries! Perhaps the most-used condiment on the farm, homemade ketchup isn't in the same category as the store-bought variety. If you have a picky eater or two who must have their favorite brand, you may not convert them. However, I've found that most who have tried homemade ketchup never look back.

PROCESSING TIME: 15 MINUTES | PRESSURE: 10 POUNDS WEIGHTED GAUGE, 11 POUNDS DIAL GAUGE
YIELD: 4 PINTS

13 pounds tomatoes, chopped

3 onions, chopped

4 cups sugar

2 cups white or apple cider vinegar, 5%

3 teaspoons salt

½ teaspoon ground cloves

½ teaspoon ground cinnamon

½ teaspoon dry mustard

½ teaspoon red pepper flakes

1. In a large stockpot over medium heat, combine the tomatoes and onions. Cook, stirring frequently, until the onions are soft.

2. Transfer the mixture to a cloth juice bag and hang above the pot or a large bowl. Let drain for 2 hours.

3. Meanwhile, prepare 4 pint jars and the canner: Clean the jars and prepare the 2-piece lids according to the manufacturer's guidelines. Keep the jars in hot but not boiling water until you're ready to use them. Prepare the canner by filling it with 2 to 3 inches of water and bringing it to a simmer, or according to your manufacturer's directions.

4. Run the drained pulp through a food mill or blend with an immersion blender to smooth out any seeds and skins. Return the smooth pulp mixture to the pot and place it over medium-high heat. Stir in the sugar, vinegar, salt, cloves, cinnamon, mustard, and red pepper flakes. Bring to a boil and boil for 10 minutes, stirring frequently.

5. Carefully ladle the hot ketchup into the hot jars, leaving ¾ inch of headspace.

6. Remove any air bubbles with a plastic or wooden utensil, adding more hot ketchup as needed to maintain the proper ¾-inch headspace.

7. Wipe the rims and seal the jars hand-tight with the 2-piece lids.

8. Carefully transfer the filled jars to the rack inside the pressure canner. Process the jars at the pressure listed above for 15 minutes.

9. Let the canner return to 0 pounds pressure. Wait 10 minutes more, then carefully open the canner lid according to the manufacturer's instructions.

10. With a jar lifter, remove the jars and place them on a clean dishtowel away from any drafts. Once the jars cool to room temperature, check the seals. If any jars have not sealed, refrigerate them and use the ketchup within 2 weeks.

CHICKEN OR TURKEY BROTH

Both chicken and turkey soup are frequent menu items on our farm. Yet I make this broth quite often because it's so useful beyond just the expected soups. A cup of broth with a pinch of cayenne pepper soothes even the worst cold. And my college-age children always ask for jars of it take back to their dorm rooms. I'm sure it ends up the base of many quick and easy dinners! Make your turkey broth after the holidays and get the most out of the bird—truly using every bit of it. For this recipe, make the broth the day before you can it so you can chill it and skim off the fat. You can use a 10- to 15-pound carcass for this or you can use cuts with meat. Just remove the meat and use it for something else after cooking instead of canning it.

PROCESSING TIME: 20 MINUTES | **PRESSURE: 10 POUNDS WEIGHTED GAUGE, 11 POUNDS DIAL GAUGE**
YIELD: 8 PINTS

3 pounds chicken or
turkey pieces

1 gallon water

2 celery stalks

2 onions, halved, skin on

15 peppercorns

3 whole bay leaves

Salt to taste

1. In a large stockpot over high heat, combine the poultry pieces and water. Bring to a boil.

2. Add the celery, onions, peppercorns, bay leaves, and salt. Reduce the heat to low and simmer, covered, for 2 hours, stirring occasionally.

3. Strain the hot broth through a cheesecloth-lined colander or fine-mesh sieve. Chill overnight.

4. The next day, remove and discard the fat layer on top before proceeding with the recipe. Reheat the broth to boiling.

5. Meanwhile, prepare 8 pint jars and the canner: Clean the jars and prepare the 2-piece lids according to the manufacturer's guidelines. Keep the jars in hot but not boiling water until you're ready to use them. Prepare the canner by filling it with 2 to 3 inches of water and bringing it to a simmer, or according to your manufacturer's directions.

6. Carefully ladle the hot broth into the hot jars, leaving 1 inch of headspace.

7. Remove any air bubbles with a plastic or wooden utensil, adding more hot broth as needed to maintain the proper 1-inch headspace.

8. Wipe the rims and seal the jars hand-tight with the 2-piece lids.

9. Carefully transfer the filled jars to the rack inside the pressure canner. Process the jars at the pressure listed above for 20 minutes.

10. Let the canner return to 0 pounds pressure. Wait 10 minutes more, then carefully open the canner lid according to the manufacturer's instructions.

(continued)

11. With a jar lifter, remove the jars and place them on a clean dishtowel away from any drafts. Once the jars cool to room temperature, check the seals. If any jars have not sealed, refrigerate them and use the broth within 1 week. Label the remaining jars with the recipe name and date before storing.

BEEF BONE BROTH

Beef broth is perfect for those cold winter meals. It's a delicious treat on its own in a mug (just salt to taste) and is the ideal base for your favorite stew. Rather than shop for this recipe, I try to save all my beef bones in the freezer, until I have enough for a batch of stock. The good news is, no bones are better than others for this recipe—save all of them! Be sure to remove any visible fat before freezing and store them in an airtight freezer bag. For this recipe, make the broth the day before you want to can it so you can chill it and skim off the fat. If you have a couple of days and a slow cooker, this recipe can be made that way as well. The flavor develops beautifully if cooked overnight.

PROCESSING TIME: 25 MINUTES | PRESSURE: 10 POUNDS WEIGHTED GAUGE, 11 POUNDS DIAL GAUGE
YIELD: 8 PINTS

3 pounds assorted beef bones

1 gallon cold water

1 large yellow onion, halved, skin on

2 garlic cloves

Salt and pepper to taste (optional)

1. In a large stockpot over high heat, combine the bones, cold water, onion, and garlic. Bring to a boil. Reduce the heat to low, cover the pot, and simmer for 4 hours. Alternatively, place all ingredients in a slow cooker set on low heat, cover the cooker, and cook for at least 8 hours, or overnight.

2. Strain the broth through a cheesecloth-lined colander or fine-mesh sieve. Taste and season with salt or pepper, if desired. Chill overnight.

3. The next day, remove and discard the fat layer on top before proceeding with the recipe. Reheat the broth to boiling.

4. Meanwhile, prepare 8 pint jars and the canner: Clean the jars and prepare the 2-piece lids according to the manufacturer's guidelines. Keep the jars in hot but not boiling water until you're ready to use them. Prepare the canner by filling it with 2 to 3 inches of water and bringing it to a simmer, or according to your manufacturer's directions.

5. Carefully ladle the hot broth into the hot jars, leaving 1 inch of headspace.

6. Remove any air bubbles with a plastic or wooden utensil, adding liquid as needed to maintain the proper 1-inch headspace.

7. Wipe the rims and seal the jars hand-tight with the 2-piece lids.

8. Carefully transfer the filled jars to the rack inside the pressure canner. Process the jars at the pressure listed above for 25 minutes.

9. Let the canner return to 0 pounds pressure. Wait 10 minutes more, then carefully open the canner lid according to the manufacturer's instructions.

10. With a jar lifter, remove the jars and place them on a clean dishtowel away from any drafts. Once the jars cool to room temperature, check the seals. If any jars have not sealed, refrigerate them and use the broth within 1 week. Label the remaining jars with the recipe name and date before storing.

GARLIC BROTH

Broth is perhaps not the most glamorous of foods to can, but it is one of the nicest things to have on the shelf. Garlic broth is my little secret for restorative dishes. My favorite thing to do for a sick family member is to serve a mug of this with a few red pepper flakes floating in it. However, you can also use it in many recipes in place of Chicken or Turkey Broth (page 177). It's a great way to make your vegetable soups vegan without sacrificing the deep flavors that meat-based broths bring to a recipe.

PROCESSING TIME: 20 MINUTES | PRESSURE: 10 POUNDS WEIGHTED GAUGE, 11 POUNDS DIAL GAUGE
YIELD: 8 PINTS

20 garlic cloves, peeled

1 gallon water

2 onions, halved, skin on

Salt and pepper to taste

1. In a large stockpot over high heat, Combine the garlic and water. Bring to a boil.

2. Add the onions and reduce the heat to low. Simmer for 2 hours, stirring occasionally.

3. Meanwhile, prepare 8 pint jars and the canner: Clean the jars and prepare the 2-piece lids according to the manufacturer's guidelines. Keep the jars in hot but not boiling water until you're ready to use them. Prepare the canner by filling it with 2 to 3 inches of water and bringing it to a simmer, or according to your manufacturer's directions.

4. Carefully strain the hot broth through a cheesecloth-lined colander. Taste, and season with salt and pepper. Return the broth to the pot and heat over high heat until it boils. Turn off the heat.

5. Carefully ladle the hot broth into the hot jars, leaving 1 inch of headspace.

6. Remove any air bubbles with a plastic or wooden utensil, adding more hot broth as needed to maintain the proper 1-inch headspace.

7. Wipe the rims and seal the jars hand-tight with the 2-piece lids.

8. Carefully transfer the filled jars to the rack inside the pressure canner. Process the jars at the pressure listed above for 20 minutes.

9. Let the canner return to 0 pounds pressure. Wait 10 minutes more, then carefully open the canner lid according to the manufacturer's instructions.

10. With a jar lifter, remove the jars and place them on a clean dishtowel away from any drafts. Once the jars cool to room temperature, check the seals. If any jars have not sealed, refrigerate them and use the broth within 1 week.

VEGETABLE BROTH

The following vegetable broth recipe is my base—but it's a bit different each time I make it when it comes to the pound and a half of vegetables. That's because, just as with the Beef Bone Broth (page 181), the base is built on extras that I stash away. I keep a freezer bag in my freezer to add to throughout the month. I throw in leftover vegetables, like half an onion, the tops of carrots, and occasionally, extras from the farmers' market. When that bag is full, I empty it in a stockpot and cover everything with water. This mix of vegetables makes a wonderful broth for many recipes. Naturally, this recipe should be the foundation of your next vegetable stew, but don't stop there. Use this broth for bean soups or try it in a recipe in place of chicken broth.

PROCESSING TIME: 20 MINUTES | PRESSURE: 10 POUNDS WEIGHTED GAUGE, 11 POUNDS DIAL GAUGE
YIELD: 4 PINTS

2 quarts water

1½ pounds assorted vegetables

2 large carrots, peeled and halved

1 celery stalk

1 onion, halved, skin on

2 garlic cloves

3 whole bay leaves

Salt and pepper to taste

1. In a large stockpot over high heat, combine all the ingredients and season with salt and pepper. Bring to a boil. Reduce the heat to low and simmer for 2 hours, stirring occasionally.

2. Meanwhile, prepare 4 pint jars and the canner: Clean the jars and prepare the 2-piece lids according to the manufacturer's guidelines. Keep the jars in hot but not boiling water until you're ready to use them. Prepare the canner by filling it with 2 to 3 inches of water and bringing it to a simmer, or according to your manufacturer's directions.

3. Carefully strain the hot broth through a cheesecloth-lined colander. Return the broth to the pot and heat over high heat until it boils. Turn off the heat.

4. Carefully ladle the hot broth into the hot jars, leaving 1 inch of headspace.

5. Remove any air bubbles with a plastic or wooden utensil, adding more hot broth as needed to maintain the proper 1-inch headspace.

6. Wipe the rims and seal the jars hand-tight with the 2-piece lids.

7. Carefully transfer the filled jars to the rack inside the pressure canner. Process the jars at the pressure listed above for 20 minutes.

8. Let the canner return to 0 pounds pressure. Wait 10 minutes more, then carefully open the canner lid according to the manufacturer's instructions.

9. With a jar lifter, remove the jars and place them on a clean dishtowel away from any drafts. Once the jars cool to room temperature, check the seals. If any jars have not sealed, refrigerate them and use the broth within 1 week.

RESOURCES

CANNING SUPPLIES

The internet makes it simple to find and buy anything you need for proper canning. Here are some of my favorite places to buy products that I actually can use and that will last.

Canning Supply: www.canningsupply.com
Pressure canners to jelly bags, you can find all of it, and things you never thought of.

Fresh Preserving: www.freshpreserving.com
For everything canning, this website from Ball is the place to go.

Kitchen Krafts: www.kitchenkrafts.com/category/home-canning-tools-and-supplies
This site has a huge inventory of canning supplies. I love it because when all other canning supply companies are backordered, Kitchen Krafts seems to come through every time.

Pressure Cooker Outlet: www.pressurecooker-outlet.com/Canning-Supplies.htm
Pressure canners that you will dream about are found at this site.

Safe Canning Practices:
nchfp.uga.edu/how/can_home.html
The National Center for Home Food Preservation is your source for current research-based recommendations for most methods of home food preservation.

nchfp.uga.edu/publications/publications_usda.html
USDA's *Complete Guide to Home Canning*. Download free. Adobe Reader 10 (or higher) is needed for proper viewing and printing of the USDA canning guide files.

Stainless Steel Screw Bands: www.Ecojarz.com
Stainless steel screw bands will last for years with careful cleaning. They will not rust and do not bend nearly as easily as the tin variety.

INDEX

ABOUT THE AUTHOR

Amelia "Amy" Jeanroy has been canning and preserving foods for twenty-five years. She is coauthor of *Canning and Preserving for Dummies* and author of *Fermenting for Dummies*, as well as hundreds of magazine articles about food preservation, homesteading, cooking, and rural living. Amy is a master gardener and has owned a greenhouse business since 2010, growing plants, produce, and seeds for farmers' markets. She has been a guest on the *Martha Stewart Living* radio show, the *Take Care* show on NPR, PBS's *Earth Eats*, and *The Wisconsin Vegetable Gardener*. Find her online as "The Farming Wife" on Facebook and YouTube.